Designing Your Teaching Life

Designing Your Teaching Life

What Student Teachers Should Know about Classrooms Today

Trace Lahey

ROWMAN & LITTLEFIELD
Lanham • Boulder • New York • London

Published by Rowman & Littlefield
An imprint of The Rowman & Littlefield Publishing Group, Inc.
4501 Forbes Boulevard, Suite 200, Lanham, Maryland 20706
www.rowman.com

6 Tinworth Street, London SE11 5AL, United Kingdom

Copyright © 2019 by Trace Lahey

All rights reserved. No part of this book may be reproduced in any form or by any electronic or mechanical means, including information storage and retrieval systems, without written permission from the publisher, except by a reviewer who may quote passages in a review.

British Library Cataloguing in Publication Information Available

Library of Congress Cataloging-in-Publication Data Available

ISBN 978-1-4758-5013-0 (cloth)
ISBN 978-1-4758-5014-7 (pbk.)
ISBN 978-1-4758-5015-4 (electronic)

This book is dedicated to all of the student teachers with whom I have worked. I remain inspired by your commitment to the noble profession of teaching.

Contents

Foreword: Ruth Vinz	ix
Preface: Designing Your Teaching Life	xv
Acknowledgments	xxiii
1 Planning for a Successful Student Teaching Experience	1
Preface to Chapters 2 and 3	17
2 Working with Your Program-Based Mentor	19
3 Working with Key School Stakeholders	33
Preface to Chapters 4 and 5	51
4 Designing High-Quality Lesson Plans	53
5 Designing a Range of High-Quality Assessments	81
6 Designing High-Quality Instruction	107
7 Analyzing and Acting on Assessment Data	125
8 Composing a Strong, Aligned edTPA	143
References: Supporting Your Student Teaching with Further Reading	165
About the Author	173

Foreword

ATTUNING TO THE *POSSIBLE*

As the story goes, a new state-of-the-art library was commissioned for a small town on the West Coast. A city council member, who was an insurance man by trade and a wannabe architect by avocation, constituted a committee to advise him on the blueprints he had drafted. The insurance man described the large, open space for a massive reading room, pointed out conference rooms for smaller meetings in one corner, and provided great detail about the design of a computer room in the center of the building (to highlight the "state-of-the-art" claim). The committee members listened intently to his blueprint tour, nodding approval throughout. Study cubicles were in abundance, positioned beneath large skylights that, as the committee was told, would give the ambience of "letting the outside in." Committee members nodded again. The blueprints were, well, beautifully blue and detailed enough to make the committee satisfied that everything had been worked out and sketched into the design for a perfect new library.

"What planning," exclaimed the council chair.

"You have thought of everything," said Ms. Meyers, the secretary of the council.

Sketches of the plumbing and electrical systems, heating and cooling systems, placement of windows and doors—the architectural nervous system and building blocks of the library—were detailed through careful hand print and line drawings. Our practicing architect stated proudly that he had consulted several books on building state-of-the-art libraries and had studied the blueprints of libraries of similar size to render his drawings. Without questions or further discussion and with much acclaim for their friend and neighbor, the committee approved the blueprints. Our insurance man, moonlighting as architect, hired a friend of a friend as the project manager. The project manager put together a team of carpenters, a plumber, and an electrician, and each followed the blueprints carefully until the edges were ragged and the blue of the prints was stained and faded. Again, it must be noted that no one asked questions about the design. As they sawed and hammered and wired the skeletal frame of the building in place, everyone followed directions. Windows and doors and skylights were tucked into their predetermined places. Everyone followed directions. The project was finished a month before the planned completion. The local newspaper documented the building from blueprint to ribbon-cutting ceremony. Books were placed on the new gleaming shelves and ten new computers were powered on (and no one asked how this was a state-of-the-art library). The library was declared a "prototype" for future libraries in surrounding towns.

Within a month, the building suffered a collapse. No one could determine a cause until the librarian said: "I was thinking when unpacking all those boxes of books and carrying them from one floor of the building to the next and from one room to another, just how heavy books are."

Ms. Meyers said, "I would never have thought of that."

The council chair added, "He consulted others' plans and renderings, so I thought the design was sound."

"Oops," said the insurance man-wannabe-architect, "I forgot to account for the weight of books." After all, our insurance man consulted books and plans for state-of-the-art libraries that relied heavily on technology and digitized holdings. Those libraries had packed up their hard copy books and taken them to off-site storage facilities. Oops. The lesson from this parable might be: The best of plans may not lead to the intended consequences. Context makes a difference, as do the books or people who will inhabit the spaces. Planning ahead is a rehearsal of what "might be" not assurances of what "will be."

TEACHING IN THE COMPANY OF OTHERS

The story of a library project gone wrong may seem a distant caution to you as a teacher in the early stages of your career. However, what you will find in the chapters that await you in *Designing Your Teaching Life* are stories, explanations, and advice from student teachers and teachers who are continuously (re)designing their professional teaching lives in response to what they learn along the way about how diverse contexts and student concerns inform their decisions, actions, and beliefs in and about teaching. The many perspectives offered to you throughout these chapters are reminders of the immense responsibilities, challenges, and exhilarations of teaching. Most importantly, what Trace Lahey emphasizes from the beginning of this book to the end is that you as a teacher are continuously learning both from your teaching and from your relationships with others—students, teachers, administrators, parents, community members, and authors of professional literature. You cannot just nod and take others' plans and advice as fitting to you and your teaching situation. You can take seriously what others say and question the assumptions and principles, turn the ideas over and around until, if useful, they become your own. You cannot design the blueprint of your teaching life by filling the page with the line drawings and design of others. You cannot passively nod at what others claim are "sound, replicable, or best practices." As we learn from our allegory of library design, it depends on the particulars and nuances of the situation. Teaching IS a restless journey not toward some anticipated perfect ending place but *ever in motion* because we are always learning and teaching in the company of others.

From the moment you enter a school building or a classroom, the ghosts of teachers past will haunt your dreams. Teachers in the rooms adjacent to yours or who serve as your cooperating teacher or co-teacher will confound or, sometimes, support your *ever-in-motion* plans. And your students' voices and actions will be with you always as you imagine alternative ways to engage students or as you respond to their work and consider what their needs might suggest about what comes next. Parents or administrators may rise up as near holograms with cautionary tales when you take flight from sanctioned instructional practices, curricular designs, or the nagging call for more test preparation. (Re)cognition in teaching is not a confrontation with self but an association with self *in relation* to others who are present or remembered as you are planning or teaching. You are never alone, not even with your thoughts. Moment by moment, hour by hour, day in and day out as the seasons and years overflow, teaching *will* keep teaching you about teaching. You see now? You, in the company of others, continuously learn about teaching and learning.

PUTTING YOUR ASPIRATIONS INTO WORDS

Trace Lahey and the teachers who share insights in this book describe aspects of the early experiences you will encounter in the first days or year of teaching. As Lahey suggests, you cannot put aside the desires, aspirations, and dreams that compose your teaching lives for the sake of technical performance. Just think for a moment how hard it is to narrate the experience of a dream when you awaken from a night's sleep. The vividness, the aliveness, and the clarity of vision fall away in the morning light. So, too, it is with dreams of teaching and learning. These are hard to put into words, and when we do, we distort and alter the vision. Here's the consequence of this conundrum: *We change the dream so it makes sense in the language we have available to us.*

This statement is important enough that I want to write it again: *We change the dream so it makes sense in the language we have available to us:* "I had this dream." The dream is reduced to a commonplace. And, sadly, the visionary experience is carried away in wisps as the sleeping brain awakens to different legacies of language. What we imagine and dream for our schools and ourselves as teachers and the students with whom we work cannot easily be put into words or, more importantly, into action. And the language we use in planning or assessments or standards is only a feeble attempt to say: "I/we have a dream."

The complexity and richness of the dream of teaching and learning is captured in curricula, standards, and assessments in the seemingly simple phrase "what students should know and be able to do." I don't know if saying this helps us know any more than we do already about understanding the level or quality of our students' work or changes in our teaching responsibilities and classrooms. Ultimately it is our classrooms that become the language, the illustration of the dream.

Hannah Arendt puts it this way: "Education is . . . where we decide whether we love our children enough not to . . . strike from their hands their chance of undertaking something new, something unforeseen by us." To help students "undertake something new," to assist them in their task of imagining the unforeseen is a good description of how I'd name my inspiration. Behind the strategies, behind the literate activities, beyond the particular texts and performances that assess and disseminate learning are some habits of mind that we, as teachers, and students as producers bring to the learning experience. While each of us would elaborate on these in different ways, I'll give my version. As Edward Said stated: "Education is not a kind of action; it is also a frame of mind, a kind of work, an attitude, a consciousness." I believe behind all the dreaming, the blueprints, and the hammering out, the purpose of education is "to create dis-ease and longing." I find a central premise for this disposition in the starkly simple quote from de Saint-Exupéry.

LONGING AND TEACHING

If you want to build a ship, don't drum up people together to collect wood and don't assign them tasks and work, but rather teach them to long for the endless immensity of the sea.

Antoine de Saint-Exupéry, *Citadelle*, 1948

Obviously, *longing* has not been one of the major dispositions or skills identified for teachers to possess, nor has *longing* been listed on a rubric or as a stated objective for student or teacher learning. And yet, as de Saint-Exupéry reminds us, if we want meaningful action or achievement, a sense of longing—to learn, to design, to imagine—is centrally important.

Longing: The concrete and unambiguous competes with surprise and risk. I feel often the gap between my belief in *longing* and the competing logic that I must teach students what others or I think they should *know*. Longing resides in restlessness, the need to keep searching for what *might be* possible in teaching and learning *with* others. I am not prescribing characteristics of longing, but I am trying to explain that there is something deeper that accompanies all the careful planning of curriculum or assessments or ways of working with colleagues, parents, students, and administrators. Your teaching life is too important to be shaped only through logics. I don't want you to forget that the teaching life you deserve and imagine should be filled with joy and speculation, knowledge, desire, creativity, and, yes, longing. Carry *longing* with you into your teaching and into the reading of this book.

Ruth Vinz, Teachers College, Columbia University

Preface

DESIGNING YOUR TEACHING LIFE

I have been a teacher for twenty-seven years, and I can still vividly recall my student teaching experience in middle school in New York City. I remember feeling intimidated by the seventh graders who sat in their desks looking at me as if they were thinking, "OK, Miss, show us what you've got," and expecting me to lead them.

I remember asking them questions about the assigned readings and getting responses that were vastly different from what I had anticipated. I had no idea what to do with those responses. As a result, I spent countless hours drafting and revising discussion questions, phrasing them precisely in order to generate the answers I was expecting.

I remember participating in parent-student conferences, and when the father of a straight A student asked my cooperating teacher what he should do to make his daughter an even better student, she replied, "Give her some chocolate every once in a while."

And I remember my last day of student teaching, when my cooperating teacher threw a little party and my students gave me a "Thank You and Good Luck" card. I cried when I left, and I can, twenty-seven years later, still recall their faces and their names.

I also remember a point when I became deeply frustrated with student teaching, especially (though unfairly) with my cooperating teacher. I suppose I got to a point where I did not think I needed anymore instruction (or *meddling*, as I saw it) from her or any of my other mentors. In fact, I wanted them to get out of my way and just let me teach.

Then I took a vacation and visited my brother.

At the time, my brother was enrolled in an architecture program. Over the years, I had listened to him describe different theories behind architectural movements, as well as the thought and planning an architect put into a building. I had stood on street corners while he pointed out architectural features, and watched his early attempts at sketching out blueprints. However, on this occasion when I visited him, he was building a 3-D model from a blueprint plan.

He showed me his blueprints and explained how much time and effort they took because of how important it was to get the scale and proportions (and other design features that I did not understand) just right. They determined whether his emerging project would succeed or fail. And as I looked at his 3-D project made out of cardboard and Styrofoam, I understood that his blueprints were actually helping him create something real. And something serious. Constructing a building is a serious endeavor. If a beam collapses, a lot of people lose a lot of money. People get hurt.

Watching my brother design a structure made me rethink my student teaching. Architects patiently and precisely craft their blueprints to ensure that their structures are sound and beautiful. I wanted to be a teacher who would design a sound and beautiful classroom, because teaching and learning is a serious endeavor also. Without a sound plan, students lose valuable learning time.

So I summoned my patience, determined to use my student teaching as an opportunity to get my teaching "blueprints" just right. And twenty-seven years later, my blueprints, those fundamental practices that link to my fundamental beliefs about teaching and learning, remain intact.

I now use the metaphor of blueprints with my own teacher education students and encourage them to articulate, track, and refine the blueprints on which they hope to design their teaching lives. And it is from this perspective that I titled this book, *Designing Your Teaching Life*.

As you read the chapters, you will be introduced to a series of topics that make up the foundation of a strong teaching practice. These include building key relationships; designing high-quality lessons, assessments, and instruction; and working with assessment data to communicate progress with students and make decisions about how and what to teach them.

Also, because so many student teachers must now prepare edTPA assessments, an endeavor that will also help you refine your blueprints, this book provides guidance for the edTPA all the way through, culminating in a chapter that details this assessment and provides specific advice to ensure your success.

THIS BOOK WAS WRITTEN FOR STUDENT TEACHERS

If you are reading this book, you have likely progressed through your teacher preparation program and are now on the verge of student teaching or you have already started student teaching. If so, you deserve to be congratulated, because you have put in countless hours striving to do well in your academic courses and at least 100 hours in schools completing field hours to earn the status of a student teacher.

As you will soon discover, student teaching, simultaneously rewarding and challenging, is more than anything, incredibly transformative. You may think of yourself as an education student right now, but by the end of your student teaching experience, you will be different.

By the time you complete student teaching, you will have created and implemented lesson plans, designed discussion questions, reviewed and commented on student work, figured out how to motivate your students, and figured out multiple ways to engage students in learning.

Also, you will know your students well. You will know about their lives and interests in and out of school, and you will know their strengths and challenges. If you are lucky, you will have met most of their parents/guardians and have a sense of their home lives and communities.

You will also possess an understanding of the struggles involved in teaching, the ethical issues that swirl around school and classroom life, the weight of your responsibilities, and mostly, the exhilarating joy of collaborating with your students. You will, at this point, likely regard yourself as a teacher who is ready to lead your own classroom.

Because you will put such a strong effort into your student teaching, it is important that you understand what a positive experience it is, and what you have to look forward to. Below are several highlights from former student teachers.

- When I was student teaching in a fourth grade class, a boy looked up at me and said, "I think adults see the world in black and white and kids see it in color." That was one of the most insightful things I ever heard, and it reminded me that we don't just teach students, students also teach us to see the world from their point of view.
- The best part of student teaching happens when you help a student to overcome an academic challenge where they have failed over and over again. Suddenly their face lights up with understanding, and you know you have done your job well.

- Getting to know your students' parents and about their home lives was powerful. It made me love them even more and, in some cases, made me realize that the best part of their day is here at school with us.
- Looking out at the students in a classroom and knowing that I have some role in the future of our society. I am helping to shape the future's doctors, lawyers, architects, engineers, and, of course, future teachers. Maybe even the next president!
- The amazing relationship I developed with the students. I cried on my last day of student teaching because they meant so much to me and I would miss them, and I knew how much I meant to them.
- Having fun in the classroom—coming up with creative ways to work with topics and materials, and to figure out how to help diverse learners learn—also just laughing with the students, who can be so fun. You get free comedy all day long.
- Sharing what I learned in my own academic studies and in the world, and watching students learn the same things.
- Student teaching just generally made me a more confident person, because I had to be prepared and I had to be a leader every day.

Over the years, I have heard many student teachers describe a singular moment that happens during student teaching. This moment often occurs when the student teacher is in the middle of a teaching task, such as working through a lesson plan or helping students transition from one activity to another. Suddenly the student teacher feels a shift. Sometimes a small shift, and other times, something larger, more dramatic.

When student teachers describe this moment, it corresponds with the realization that the classroom landscape has changed somehow. It feels and even looks different than before, more familiar somehow. And in this moment, the student teacher feels different too. They no longer feel like a student visitor from the outside, they feel like a teacher. Like *the* teacher who is "running the show" and to whom the students look to for support, advice, and leadership. So look out for this special moment, and when it happens . . . enjoy it.

THE AIM OF THIS BOOK

The aim of this book is to provide guidance on many aspects of your student teaching experience. It is a good idea to read this book before you start student teaching, so that you gain a strong understanding of what is ahead for you, and then to return to consider relevant sections as they come up in your student teaching.

This book will provide support along the way in the form of in-depth, detailed advice. The advice included in this book has been collected from teacher-educators in teacher preparation programs, college-based clinical supervisors, former student teachers, and from cooperating teachers and school administrators who work with student teachers in schools. Advice and examples are directed at a variety of disciplines and grade levels in order to make the book relevant to most student teachers. As stated earlier, this book is also geared to support your edTPA preparations if you live in a state that requires the edTPA for certification.

This book highlights key issues in student teaching by presenting them through narrative accounts of real student teaching situations in order to bring some of the central topics to life. No two student teaching contexts are the same, but the narrative accounts in this book are intended to invite readers to examine the presented topics in depth, and also to connect imaginatively (How might you handle the situation?) as well as emotionally (How might you feel in a similar situation?).

THE BOOK'S STRUCTURE

Chapter 1: Planning for a Successful Student Teaching Experience

This chapter will provide you with guidance intended to help you organize your life for the student teaching experience. It includes advice from cooperating teachers and former student teachers to help you navigate your first days as a student teacher, addressing topics such as:

- What can you expect on your very first day?
- How will things go the first week?
- What are some conversations that you can prepare for?
- What are some potential challenges you might encounter and how can you deal with those challenges?

Chapters 2 and 3 focus on the professional relationships you will build while student teaching, offering narratives that bring to life the importance of remaining proactive, positive, and professional so that you can successfully network in your school and get the support you need from those with whom you will work during your student teaching experience.

Chapter 2: Working with Your Program-Based Mentor

This chapter introduces you to the role of your program-based mentor(s), highlights the importance of establishing strong communication with your program-based mentors, and offers advice about how to prepare for your program-based evaluations, including your teaching observations.

Chapter 3: Working with Key School Stakeholders

This chapter builds on the idea that the relationships you form during student teaching will be important to your success and highlights ways in which your relationships with your school-based mentors and others, especially students, will support your student teaching. The chapter also points out potential pitfalls that can deter your progress.

Chapter 4: Designing High-Quality Lesson Plans

Having a strong plan is essential. Even if your cooperating teacher doesn't write down plans, he or she likely has all of the lesson-plan features "in their head." This chapter will help you understand the many elements of instructional design that you need to consider when planning, and offers suggestions about how to work effectively with (and around) scripted curricula. This chapter is also designed to support student teachers in writing comprehensive, aligned, and differentiated lesson plans that can be used as edTPA artifacts or other student teaching portfolio materials.

Chapter 5: Designing a Range of High-Quality Assessments

This chapter describes how teachers plan a range of high-quality, aligned, and differentiated assessments. In this chapter, you will learn how to design and implement a variety of assessments in order to plan, monitor, and evaluate student learning.

Chapter 6: Designing High-Quality Instruction

This chapter details what it takes to successfully implement your instructional plans. Common characteristics and practices that support positive classroom environments, engaged students, academic discourse, differentiated instruction, and explicit instruction are presented.

This chapter also provides questions for student teachers to consider when they reflect on their instruction so that they can continue to improve. In addition, the chapter offers a rationale for recording your teaching and guidance for those student teachers who are required to produce video recordings for the edTPA or their student teaching portfolios.

Chapter 7: Analyzing and Acting on Assessment Data

In this chapter you will learn how to create data from your assessments, portray and analyze assessment results, provide aligned and thoughtful feedback, and identify learning goals for your students based on your assessment data. Student teachers will be provided with step-by-step guidance, assessment examples, and questions for reflection around the challenge of assessment. This chapter will prepare candidates for Task 3 of the edTPA.

Chapter 8: Composing a Strong, Aligned edTPA

This chapter is for the candidate who is preparing an edTPA. Building on the guidance provided throughout the book, this chapter offers a comprehensive description of the assessment, as well as advice and checklists for each of the required tasks.

REFERENCES: SUPPORTING YOUR STUDENT TEACHING WITH FURTHER READING

The references include resources that are organized to complement the topics presented in this book. The suggested materials will help support your planning, instruction, assessment, and reflection during student teaching and beyond.

OTHER KEY ELEMENTS FOR YOUR BLUEPRINTS

In addition to providing guidance focused on the topics described above, discussions about the importance of alignment, evidence-based instruction, differentiation, diversity, academic language, and the value of reflection are woven throughout the book. Look out for these discussions; they deserve special consideration, as they are elements you will want to include in your blueprints for effective teaching.

If you work mindfully through the student teaching experience while reflecting frequently on your work with students and curriculum, you will be able to apply much of your learning to your future classroom. That will benefit you not just in your first year but also in the years to come. Student teaching is the ideal time to intentionally lay down your blueprints, designing the practices that will sustain you and your students.

To sum up, reflect on the following quote from Dr. Martin Luther King Jr. and get ready to start designing your blueprints.

I want to ask you a question, and that is: What is your life's blueprint? Whenever a building is constructed, you usually have an architect who draws a blueprint, and that blueprint serves as the pattern, as the guide, . . . and a building is not well erected without a good, sound, and solid blueprint.

Now each of you is in the process of building the structure of your lives, and the question is: whether you have a proper, a solid, and a sound blueprint.[2]

NOTES

1. American Association of Colleges for Teacher Education, http://edtpa.aacte.org.
2. Dr. Martin Luther King Jr., "The 50th Anniversary of Martin Luther King, Jr.'s, 'What Is Your Life's Blueprint?,'" Beacon Broadside (Beacon Press: October 2016), https://www.beaconbroadside.com/broadside/2017/10/the-50th-anniversary-of-martin-luther-king-jrs-what-is-your-lifes-blueprint.html, accessed January 22, 2019.

Acknowledgments

I would like to thank my family for their strong and constant support, my colleagues for their guidance and wisdom, and my students for their dedication and idealism.

Chapter One

Planning for a Successful Student Teaching Experience

Teaching is a profession in which you will dedicate yourself to caring for your students and serving their needs. Caring for and serving the needs of others requires an incredible amount of energy, so student teaching is the perfect time to learn how to balance your professional responsibilities with other responsibilities in your life. This is an ability that will help you sustain a long and healthy teaching life.

Student teachers require sufficient time and space to successfully complete all that is demanded of them. Ensure that you create enough time to travel to and from your school and other locations where you have commitments. Ensure that you create enough time to successfully complete both your student teaching duties and your teacher preparation program's requirements. And ensure that you create enough time to take care of yourself—rest, exercise, and leisure time will ensure that you bring your best self to the work of student teaching.

Most teacher preparation programs require the student teacher to work in a school full-time for at least one semester, so count on your student teaching experience to be one of the busiest times of your life. In many cases the student teacher will have other responsibilities in addition to student teaching. This includes working, taking other classes, preparing for the edTPA, other exams, and various family obligations, so it will be important for you to figure out how to manage your time.

Consider how you will set yourself up for success when student teaching. What plans can you make to ensure that you have time and the space to successfully manage your travel and workload? Is there one change you can make that will give you more time and space? Is there a method or habit that you have already implemented that you want to make sure you continue in order to successfully student teach?

This chapter provides you with advice from former student teachers about how to set yourself up for success *before* you start student teaching and during the early days of student teaching, so that you can successfully create time and space for yourself and successfully navigate the start of your student teaching.

The following advice comes from former student teachers who were asked to reflect on their student teaching experiences. The tips below were selected because they are frequently offered words of wisdom, and student teachers have stated that they have found this advice helpful.

Tip #1: Make sure that you leave plenty of time in the morning to get to school. You do not want to be late.

College students frequently describe staying up late in order to complete classwork, therefore sleeping only a few hours before getting up to start the day or sleeping through the morning and getting up in the afternoon. If this is your regular schedule, try to break it before you start student teaching. Now you will be following a professional educator's schedule.

If your student teaching school day starts at 8:05 every morning, which is common, you will need to be in the building by 7:50 at the latest every day to help your cooperating teacher set up and to get your mind-set focused on the duties ahead.

Every so often a student teacher drops out of student teaching because he or she simply cannot get up early and arrive on time, and then they feel they wasted time in teacher education courses, just because they cannot wake up early. Tardiness will not be tolerated by your support team, and if you are consistently late, that will become a negative issue for you.

Use your winter or summer break, or two weeks prior to the start of your student teaching, to readjust your schedule so that you can get to bed early and get up early enough to make it to your school on time. Once you have this schedule down, you will have it for life, and you will need that, because that is the schedule of a teacher.

Tip #2: Figure out how to get some sleep every night. That can be challenging, but it's important. You will get tired during student teaching.

Also on the theme of sleep, this advice relates to the prior tip. Student teaching is demanding, and you will be using a great deal of energy every day to support your students, learn your profession, and fulfill your school obligations and college requirements. Student teachers generally grow increasingly tired as the semester progresses, so pace yourself and take care of yourself by getting rest when you can.

Tip #3: Make sure that you practice your route to and from your school and that you have an alternate way to get there in case the first route doesn't work out.

Consider Cindy's[1] story: Cindy had been arriving at her school almost thirty to forty minutes late nearly every day of student teaching during her first two weeks. As a strong, diligent, and professional student, her college mentors couldn't even imagine Cindy having a problem with tardiness until the school's administrator called the seminar instructor. At this point, he was frustrated and had lost his patience. "This is a real problem," he told the seminar instructor. "We are not going to let her continue to student teach if she is late nearly every day."

When the instructor confronted Cindy with the issue, Cindy described how she left her house at the same time every day, but the bus was always packed with riders and slow, so she was always late. "Well, you'll have to leave your house earlier!" the instructor cried.

"If I leave the house earlier, I can't help my younger sister get ready for school, and my parents really need my help."

The instructor showed Cindy how to access Google Maps. Cindy had not used this app before, but when her instructor plugged in her home address and the school address, they located three alternative routes that Cindy could take to school. She could take an express bus just five minutes earlier and transfer at a point closer to her school, or she could walk an additional five minutes, jump on a subway, and then catch a bus that would take her a block away from the school. The instructor recalled that another student teacher was working in the same building but in a different school, so Cindy made contact with that student teacher, and he agreed to pick her up near the subway station on his way to his school.

Once Cindy communicated her transportation issues to her college instructor, she found resources to support her commute. However, by this point, the school administrator was not inclined to give Cindy a strong recommendation, and her cooperating teacher assigned her a poor grade because of her initial tardiness. The student teaching placement was not long enough for them to get over their initial impression of Cindy.

Cindy's story illustrates how not taking initiative and communicating her dilemma to her mentors, and not taking the time prior to student teaching to figure out the best way to get to school, negatively impacted her student teaching experience. It would have been in Cindy's interest to be more proactive in this regard.

Your college has likely placed you in a school that is not ridiculously far from your home, but you will probably have to drive or take public transportation every day, unless you are very lucky and live within walking distance. Student teachers working in urban areas such as New York City rely on the subway or buses and realize that there can be serious delays in the tunnels or on roads, so they know they need to have two or even three alternative ways to get to their schools.

It is smart to have an alternate route established before student teaching starts so that if a transportation glitch occurs, you can circumvent it and get to class on time. Related to this is the parking issue that many schools have. Do not assume that parking will be easy at your school. Find out in advance where the teachers at your school park and when they must arrive in the neighborhood or the parking lot to get a spot.

Work all of this out well in advance to prevent unnecessary tardiness and stress for yourself. Consider carpooling or traveling with other student teachers working in your school or neighborhood so that you can support one another. Just remember that your students probably live close to the school, and they will be there waiting for you . . . and so will your cooperating teacher and administrator.

Tip # 4: Make sure that you figure out your schedule in advance so that you have plenty of time for student teaching, lesson planning, grading papers, and working on your edTPA or other course assignments.

It is an unfortunate reality that most student teachers have to cut down on their work schedules and only work on weekends in order to student teach, or even quit their jobs for a semester. This can be an economic hardship for many, so you will need to figure out how to ask for or apply for support (student loans/grants) if need be. If you have young children, you will need to ask for help with them and figure out a clear, reliable schedule for their care, as well as a backup in case a child is sick.

If you were planning on taking more than one additional college class with student teaching, discuss that with an advisor. It is generally not a great idea to load up on college classes during student teaching. You won't have much time to attend classes or complete the coursework. In addition, if you participate in other activities that are demanding, such as a college sports team, discuss your schedule with your coach and advisor. You need to be available to student teach, and you need to have plenty of time to prepare lesson plans and coursework, review student work, and prepare for certification exams.

Tip #5: Before you start student teaching, get your life in order. If you need to break up with someone, do it before student teaching. If you need to address family or friend problems, do that before student teaching. You do not want any drama in your life at this time.

This advice probably seems extreme, but it is remarkable how often former student teachers underscore the importance of "no drama." Perhaps that is because student teaching will take a lot out of you. The demands of showing up on time every day with a plan, giving your students 100 percent of your attention and energy, and then reviewing student work, devising new plans for the following day, and then heading to your own class to work on your edTPA or other college requirements will put a good amount of stress on you (mostly good, challenging stress).

You will enjoy your work and likely be very happy to engage in all aspects of student teaching, but other areas of your life may need to be put on hold until you get used to the demanding schedule of a teacher (and don't worry, you will get used to it).

So put every other aspect of your life in order before you begin to student teach. Let your friends and family know how your semester will be, and let them know that you will need their strong support to succeed. If you feel that you have people in your life who will not support you, deal with that before student teaching so that you are not taxing yourself further with "drama." This advice is crucial, and its importance cannot be overstated.

Tip #6: On your first day of student teaching, be prepared to sit in the school office for a while because the administrator may be too busy to greet you and bring you to your classroom. Don't take it personally. You'll get there.

You will soon learn that schools are exceedingly busy places and the needs of the students in the school come first. Your needs as a student teacher are certainly important, but they are further down on the priority list of the school administration and your cooperating teacher. Therefore, expect that, at some point during student teaching, you will have to wait to be greeted by administration, to have forms signed, etc. However, it will be good practice to learn patience and to learn how to take initiative in order to get your needs met. These two dispositions will help you as a teacher.

Consider Uzma's story: Uzma arrived for her spring semester placement on the first day of February. She was excited to get started, but nervous also. Her college instructor had told her to arrive at the school by 7:45 sharp and report to the main office. Her instructor had advised Uzma that she would then meet the school principal and be directed to her classroom, where she would meet her cooperating teacher and her students.

So Uzma introduced herself in the main office. She was told to sit and wait until the school secretary could give her a time card and show her how to use it. After she punched in with her new time card, Uzma was instructed to wait for the principal, who was in her office.

Uzma observed three families come in to get information. The principal came out of her office, greeted each family, and answered questions. One student delivered a note from a teacher, and the principal ran out of the office in response. When she got back, she had to deal with a student who had been sent to her because he had thrown a shoe across the classroom. When he was sent back to class with a tear-stained face, Uzma thought it might be her turn.

However, Uzma watched the principal zoom out of her office with a walkie-talkie. Apparently there was a flood in the basement and she had to attend to that. A half-hour later, the principal ran up to her office and declared that the three buses she had requested for a field trip were running late and the third graders would have to be moved from the cafeteria, where they were waiting to load up onto the buses, and go back to their classrooms until the buses were closer. The principal ran out of the office to help the teachers organize and move the students. Then the principal came back into the office (out of breath) and greeted Uzma. She apologized that it had taken her so long to do so.

The principal then told Uzma that she was excited to have her working at the school, especially since she had learned from the college supervisor that Uzma was an excellent student. The principal asked Uzma if she spoke any languages other than English. When Uzma revealed that she was indeed trilingual, the principal assigned her to a class in which there were several newly arrived Bengali students. Uzma would be able to support them and their teacher. The principal walked Uzma to her classroom, introduced her to her students and cooperating teacher, and Uzma was launched into student teaching at that moment. Even with a slow start, Uzma proved an incredible asset in classroom and had a positive, educational experience.

At the end of the semester, when Uzma wanted to speak to the principal to request a letter of recommendation as well as to be considered for employment as a substitute teacher at the school, she brought some schoolwork to keep her occupied while she waited for the principal to have a free moment.

This story illustrates how busy school personnel are—even if you have an appointment scheduled with a school principal, be prepared for an issue to arise that will require your patience. Remember that in schools, the students and their safety always come first.

So is this what you can expect on your very first day of student teaching? Maybe. In some cases, student teachers go to their schools for the first day without having met or communicated with their cooperating teacher. In these cases, the school administrator has committed to accepting a student teacher, has designated a cooperating teacher for the student teacher, and plans to make introductions on the first day the student teacher arrives. This is especially true in the fall if the student teacher is arriving on the first day of school.

Tip #7: Plan for time to go by faster than usual during student teaching.

Ask any former student teacher, and they will confirm that time does go by faster than usual during student teaching. It may be because student teaching is exciting and involves so much work (mostly fun work) that the time seems to fly by. This is a positive thing because it means that you will be teaching in your own classroom before you know it, but it is important to make good use of the time and to take advantage of every opportunity in student teaching that presents itself. Here are some examples:

If school personnel express an interest in supporting you by offering to observe or help you plan a lesson, take advantage of that. If the school administrator invites you to participate in after-school professional development, take advantage of that. If the media specialist invites you to come to the library and investigate research databases made available to students, take advantage of that. If the school's athletic director invites you to observe or help out during basketball games, take advantage of that too. A teacher's daily duties extend well beyond the classroom, so it is important for you to gain experience in a wide variety of activities, and to get as much support and advice as you can from anyone who offers it.

The challenging part about how quickly time goes during student teaching is that you will need to be very organized about your assignments and student teaching requirements. Many former student teachers have described how difficult it is to get back on track if they fall behind on an assignment. There is a snowball effect that happens, as most assignments build off of other assignments (this is especially true for the edTPA preparations). And because the student teacher has to balance the coursework with the schoolwork (responding to student papers, preparing materials and lesson plans), staying on top of deadlines is crucial.

Tip #8: Take initiative from the very first day. Offer to help out by working with small groups or individuals. Offer to grade papers, help with the bulletin board—anything that you see that needs to be done.

Don't just sit there and wait for your cooperating teacher to tell you what to do. Jump in. This advice builds on the previous tip, and it is amazing how often one hears this. There is much to be done in a school, and your administrator or cooperating teacher may be too busy to even think about delegating jobs that need to be done. So take initiative and jump in. Look around and see what needs to be done, and *offer to help*. This is a crucial habit to develop and will ensure that you become a valued member of any school team during student teaching and in the future.

Tip #9: Make sure that you follow the advice of your mentors. They know a lot about student teaching and will set you up for success.

This advice is self-explanatory but worth highlighting and digging into a bit. The big idea here is, make good use of your mentors. This means taking their advice seriously. Here is an example:

Your student teaching seminar instructor will likely recommend that you begin student teaching by observing your class and then slowly assuming more responsibilities so that you can teach your cooperating teacher's full schedule by your last week. If this is the recommendation, make sure that you follow that advice and share it with your cooperating teacher.

If you don't act on this advice, you might find that you have not had enough practice leading the whole class before your student teaching placement is over, or you might start teaching before you have some familiarity with the students in the room, and you might get off to a rocky start that rattles you and undermines your confidence.

If you don't understand an instruction or piece of advice, clarify that with your mentor. For example, if you are charged with helping a group of students complete a graphic organizer, make sure you understand the process your cooperating teacher wants you to use and the learning objectives that connect with the activity. You don't want to be unclear and then lead your group of students in the wrong direction. It is crucial to ask questions if you don't fully understand a direction or requirement.

Your college and school-based mentors are working as mentors because they want to support you and your future students. Also, they are experts in the field of teaching and learning, so be assured that they will be thrilled to address your questions.

Tip #10: If possible, try to contact your cooperating teacher before student teaching begins.

In some cases, student teachers are introduced to their cooperating teachers via email before their placement actually begins. If you are lucky enough to be given access to your cooperating teacher before the school year or the placement begins, write and introduce yourself and also offer to start early. If you are student teaching in the fall, offer to help your cooperating teacher set up his or her classroom. This will allow you to meet your cooperating teacher before the chaos of the first days of school and to learn how to set up a classroom. It will also demonstrate to the cooperating teacher, school administrator, and your other mentors that you take initiative.

Consider Faith's story: Because she was the only health education student in her college program, Faith learned who her cooperating teacher would be in early August, almost an entire month before she was scheduled to begin student teaching. Faith got her cooperating teacher's email from her seminar instructor and contacted him in order to introduce herself and thank him for agreeing to work with her.

Faith's cooperating teacher, Mr. Hewitt, had served as a cooperating teacher, mentoring student teachers for many years. He was thrilled to have a new student teacher assigned to him. Mr. Hewitt invited Faith to meet him at school in the summer, where he provided her with the teacher's edition textbook that he used with students and a copy of the semester-long curriculum. So Faith was able to study the curriculum in advance.

As August came to an end, Mr. Hewitt invited Faith to help him set up the classroom for the first day of school and attend pre-service, faculty professional development sessions. Faith was able to count all of those hours toward her student teaching requirement. She also got an in-depth view of how teachers set up their rooms and prepare for the first day of school. Also, when the students arrived on campus, Faith felt somewhat familiar with her curriculum, her surroundings, her cooperating teacher, and other school personnel. This, she asserted, made her feel more confident about getting started.

Not every cooperating teacher will be able to meet you in advance, as they are always very busy, but this story illustrates how, if you are able to make prior contact, it will put your mind at ease, provide you with a bit of a head start, and demonstrate your initiative to your cooperating teacher early on.

Tip #11: Communicate your program requirements with your cooperating teacher as soon as you can.

In the early days of your student teaching placement, it is a good idea to bring your student teaching materials, such as your program handbook and your edTPA handbook (if you are preparing the edTPA), to have as handy references for you and the school personnel.

During one of your first meetings with your cooperating teacher, you should highlight important requirements that you need to meet for your program/edTPA, such as any video recording that you have to record (and get permission slips for), lesson plans that you need to create, and any assessments you need to administer. Even if you are planning to teach and record full lessons during the fifth week of student teaching, tell your cooperating teacher as soon as possible.

It is also very important that you share your progression requirements with your cooperating teacher. In other words, if your program expectations are that you are teaching at least one full class by the second week of school and teaching full days by your last week, your cooperating teacher needs to know that. And don't assume that these requirements have been shared by your college program or that your cooperating teacher has had the time to review those requirements. It will be most efficient if they hear it from you.

Tip #12: It is a good idea to ease into the student teaching so that you can get to know the class.

If you are required by your seminar instructor to begin your student teaching placement by first observing the class for a few days, plan to do that. And also, ask your cooperating teacher if you can look at student work and help review or evaluate student assessments. This is not busywork. In fact, you will learn a great deal about your students' abilities and interests when you review their work.

Within a few days of starting, you should be working to support individual students and groups of students in the classroom rather than just observing. Again, this will help you learn about your students and encourage the development of relationships with your students, which will prove invaluable when you teach the whole class.

Tip #13: If you have serious problems with your cooperating teacher or placement, notify your college mentors as soon as possible.

Be assured that the process of beginning student teaching goes smoothly 99.7 percent of the time. On rare occasions however, student teachers will encounter unexpected challenges. These generally relate to cooperating teachers being assigned to student teachers with very little understanding of what that job entails. Serving as a cooperating teacher is a huge responsibility and time commitment. And just because someone is a wonderful teacher does not mean that they are a great mentor.

Some rare but challenging situations include the cooperating teacher backing out because it seems like too much of a time commitment, the cooperating teacher's refusal to let the student teacher teach the entire group of students, the cooperating teacher refusing to let the student teacher record their video, the cooperating teacher refusing to observe and debrief the student teacher, or the cooperating teacher refusing to help the student teacher with lesson planning. If any of these issues arise, make sure to communicate with your college mentors as soon as possible.

Consider Martin's story: Martin had absolutely insisted that he student teach in the school across from his home. Martin was a full-time college student who was also working full time in the neighborhood, and he could not commute to another school, he asserted. Martin had also completed most of his field hours in this same school, and he felt most comfortable there. He was certain that if the school had an opening in the near future, he would be considered for it.

His college instructor told Martin that his program had not sent student teachers to that particular school because the school's principal had told her that they were too busy preparing for state tests to take on student teachers. She had offered him a placement at a nearby school, but Martin refused.

Martin then contacted the school principal and received permission from the principal. The principal agreed because he knew and liked Martin. This persuaded his college instructor, who allowed Martin to student teach in the school. Within a few days of starting, however, Martin complained that his cooperating teacher did not seem particularly interested in helping him and had even complained that she did not really want to be responsible for the paperwork that came with student teaching. She was too busy preparing her students for the state tests.

After two weeks, the cooperating teacher contacted the college instructor. "I quit," she proclaimed. "The principal forced this on me, and I don't want a student teacher. I am sorry, and it's nothing against Martin, but I won't do it anymore." Fortunately, the seminar instructor found another placement for Martin, in the other school. It required an additional twenty minutes each day of commuting time for Martin, but it was a school that had actively accepted and mentored students from Martin's program. Martin was assigned to work with a veteran cooperating teacher who understood his program's requirements, an amazing mentor. Martin did not complain again about his commute. He realized it was worth it.

Stories like Martin's are rare and represent a worst-case scenario. But Martin's case illustrates that if difficult issues arise, your college-based mentors need to be notified right away. If need be, and in extreme situations, they will step in to find you another placement, and it is appropriate for them to do so. You will not have to handle these kinds of challenging situations alone.

Additionally, if you make sure to communicate clearly and early about what is required of you to your cooperating teacher, you and your mentors will likely be able to address any problems before too much time goes by.

Tip #14: Work hard to get to know your student teaching context. It will pay off for you.

It is likely that you have completed assignments in your methods courses in which you describe the context in which you completed your field observations. You will want to pay close attention to the context in which you will student teach as well, because the community, school, classroom, and particular group of students with whom you will work must be taken into account when you interact in the school, when you lesson plan, when you provide instruction, when you communicate with parents/guardians, and when you assess your students.

If you are preparing the edTPA, you will need to gather information about your student teaching context and describe the context in Task 1A (Context for Learning). Whether or not you are preparing for the edTPA (or a similar assignment for your student teaching seminar), you will need to gain a strong understanding of the school, and also the district and neighborhood, so that you understand what makes the community, neighborhood, school, and the classroom unique.

You will want to understand the specific curriculum used by the school or teacher. You will also want to understand special classroom features such as how students are grouped, as well as classroom rules and routines. And most important, you will need a deep understanding of the learners in your classroom.

For example, you will likely have classified students with IEPs (Individualized Education Program) or 504 plans, students with special linguistic needs such as emergent bilingual students (or students who speak a variant of English that is not considered academic English), struggling students, advanced students, or students with learning preferences that may require some accommodations or modifications. Your cooperating teacher will be able to provide you with information about the students in your class, and you will also learn about them by engaging with them and observing them closely.

In order to gain an understanding of your student teaching context, you might start by researching community demographics online. Real estate sites like trulia.com or zillow.com are especially helpful. In addition, the school district may publish "report card" statistics about the school on their website.

Also, make use of the school personnel you will encounter, including administrators, teachers, media specialists, office personnel, the parent coordinator, custodians, and security officers, just to name a few. They will tell you a lot about your teaching context.

Below is a list of questions to help you better understand your student teaching context.

Community, Cultural, and District Factors

- How would you describe the geographic location, the community, and the school population's socioeconomic profile, languages, and race/ethnicity?
- How would you describe the stability of community, local political climate, community support for education, historical significance, and other environmental factors?
- How would you describe resources that the community and school provide for people and students who live there that might directly or indirectly affect teaching and learning?

School Factors

- How would you describe the physical plant and discuss how you think the school's layout affects school life (such as routines and transitions)?
- How would you describe the school curriculum and forces that drive curricular decisions (for example, constant preparation for high-stakes testing or a progressive philosophy)?
- Review the school's mission statement. What does it reveal to you?
- What are some challenges the school is grappling with?
- What are some of the school's points of pride or strengths?

Classroom Factors

- What examples of the implicit curriculum do you observe in your student teaching classroom (what values are being communicated to students in ways that are not explicitly stated, such as the way seating is arranged or the messages conveyed by materials on the walls)?
- How would you describe the availability of technology equipment, resources, and the extent of parental involvement?
- What are some rules/procedures and transitions used in the class?
- How are students grouped?
- How is time scheduled?
- How does the classroom atmosphere affect teaching and learning?

Student Factors

Interview your cooperating teacher and students to learn about these topics:

- Describe the student characteristics that one must consider when designing instruction and assessment for the specific students in the class. Include factors such as age, gender, race/ethnicity, special needs, achievement/developmental levels, culture, languages, interests, learning preferences, or students' cognitive, social, and emotional skill levels.
- How does the teacher determine learning goals for the students?
- How does the teacher modify/adapt instructional plans and assessments for specific individuals or groups of students?

Instructional Implications

Once you have a sense of your student teaching context, consider how your context will influence your instruction, planning, and assessment. You won't just be teaching a generic classroom of students, you will be teaching a particular group in a particular context, so you will want to consider (and get some guidance from your cooperating teacher and other school personnel) how you will appropriately support and challenge the students in this classroom. Make sure to consider implications for diverse student learners. Make sure to consider how you will lead students toward academic and social/emotional learning.

For example, if you have several emergent bilingual students in your classroom, you will need to support them in specific ways to help them learn academic English while challenging them to learn the content you are teaching, and to consider their social and emotional needs. If you have a group of gifted and talented students in your classroom, you will want to make sure that you challenge them appropriately, so that they don't get bored and restless, but also support their unique social and emotional needs.

Considering the topics above will not only support your edTPA/student seminar assignment preparations it will support your work as a student teacher because it is crucial to understand the specific needs and strengths of the community, school, and students you will serve.

**Tip #15: Be clear about your goals and desires for student teaching. Reminding yourself of why you are doing this
will help keep you going through the amazingly fun but
also challenging times.**

REFLECTING ON THE CHAPTER

Prior to the start of your student teaching placement, reflect on the following questions. You might even share some of your thinking with other student teachers and/or your mentors.

- Why do you want to student teach?
- What are you looking forward to?
- What unique strengths are you bringing to the experience?
- What are you worried about?
- How might you address these concerns?

NOTE

1. All names in this book are pseudonyms.

Preface to Chapters 2 and 3

In schools, teaching and learning activities mainly occur in the social nexus, so strong communication skills are essential to a successful student teaching experience. If you are someone who develops relationships easily, has strong networking and communication skills, and habitually takes initiative in social situations, you won't have to work so hard at the social aspect of student teaching. If, however, you consider yourself shy or introverted (don't worry, many teachers do), you will have to work harder to "put yourself out there."

With practice, you will become a skilled navigator of professional relationships and communication with others, and you won't remember a time when this felt difficult. However, even if you are extroverted and thrive on social interaction, you will find that student teaching requires you to engage in countless interactions with people and make numerous decisions every day, so you will want to intentionally build strong communication skills and habits, anticipating potential pitfalls and thinking ahead about how best to engage with and get the support of others.

During student teaching you will place a strong emphasis on building relationships with the key people with whom you will interact when student teaching. That includes your program-based mentors such as your student teaching seminar instructor—your school-based mentors, and other school personnel whose support will be crucial. And, of course, this includes the students with whom you will work. Also, student teachers are usually invited to participate in school events that will involve parents/guardians, so try to take advantage of these opportunities so that you can get some experience communicating with parents/guardians as well.

The next two chapters provide you with advice to help you establish and maintain positive relationships with key people with whom you will interact.

Narratives from the student teaching classroom will be woven throughout to illustrate some of the challenges that can come up in student teaching, and to demonstrate how these key individuals, and especially your program-based and school-based mentors, can support you. The narratives highlight why it is crucial to communicate effectively with them.

Chapter Two

Working with Your Program-Based Mentor

In this book, the term "program" refers to the institution you are enrolled in while taking your teacher preparation courses, including student teaching. This might be a college or university program or another type of teacher education program, such as one affiliated with your district or the city where you live.

When you student teach, the program will assign one or more mentors to support you. In some programs, there is one person who will provide all of your mentoring (including teaching your student teaching seminar), and in other programs the mentoring is divided up into several roles and distributed to more than one individual. The term "program-based mentor" will be used in this book to describe the person or persons affiliated with your program who will support you during student teaching.

It is crucial that you maintain a positive relationship with your program-based mentor because he or she has a great deal of professional knowledge and can be quite helpful. This person will assign you a grade for student teaching and determine whether you can progress from your student teaching to becoming a teacher.

WHAT YOUR PROGRAM-BASED MENTOR DOES

- Your program-based mentor serves as a direct link between the school where you are student teaching and your teacher preparation program. They will likely place you at the school and communicate with your school administrator and cooperating teacher about your progress.
- Your program-based mentor has the "big picture" view of the student teaching program, arranges the student teaching placements, has ongoing

relationships with school administrators and teachers, provides an orientation for the student teachers, organizes the student teaching experience, and provides the final, overall grade for the student teaching course after communicating with the student teacher's other mentors.
- Your program-based mentor reviews your lesson plans, visits you at the school, observes your teaching, completes evaluations of your teaching, provides you with coaching, and will assign you a grade for the lessons they review and observe.
- Your program-based mentor will lead your student teaching class, organize your related college-based assignments, and provide you guidance for the edTPA and other certification exams.
- Your program-based mentor will organize your experience, providing you with readings to support your student teaching, and possibly assigning and evaluating your student teaching reflections and instructional plans. Your program-based mentor will also lead class discussions on relevant topics such as classroom management.
- Your program-based mentor is the person to go to when you have questions about your placement, your student teaching schedule, course assignments, and any issues you run into regarding your relationship with your other mentors.
- Your program-based mentor will provide you with information and workshops that may be necessary for you to meet college and state requirements. When you student teach, you are not just working toward your teacher preparation program requirements, you are working toward state requirements as well, and this person understands that "big picture."

Plan to Communicate Frequently with Your Program-Based Mentor

In addition to learning about the logistics involved in your student teaching, it is important that you communicate with your program-based mentor frequently about your student teaching progress. This person will be your advocate during student teaching, so build a relationship with him or her, not only by speaking and acting professionally but also by frequently checking in. Stop by before or after your seminars or email to let them know how your experience is going and to ask any individual questions you have about the program or your experiences.

Your program-based mentor wants to know what you are excited about, what you think you are good at, what special events are happening at the school, and how your relationships are going with your mentors and students.

Communicate frequently and honestly—strive to remain positive and use "I" messages in your communications. For example, "I am confused about that feedback," rather than "You confused me with that feedback." And strive to remain professional in all of your interactions with your mentor, including professional speech and actions.

In addition, if you have any difficulties at your site, communicate with your program-based mentor as well, and make sure that you do so early. This is important information for your mentor to have, and if they are used to interacting with you, they will likely be even more responsive if you have a problem that you need help with. This idea is illustrated below in Naima's story.

Naima's Story

Naima was student teaching in a chemistry class at a large, urban high school. She had noticed that during passing periods, high school boys would frequently yell slurs of a sexual nature at girls as they passed by. The frequency and intensity of this situation struck Naima as problematic and made her feel uncomfortable as well.

Naima shared this with her cooperating teacher, who told her that, unfortunately, it was just a part of the school's culture. Soon a boy enrolled in Naima's fourth period class started asking her personal questions and suggesting they go on "a date." Naima told her cooperating teacher. Her cooperating teacher did offer Naima the option to "sit out" fourth period, but Naima felt she would not have this option when leading her own class, so she did not opt out. The cooperating teacher reprimanded the boy. However, his behavior did not stop; it just became more subtle and therefore difficult to "catch."

For several weeks, Naima did not share any of this with her program-based mentor because she figured there was nothing that her mentor could do. But after trying to deal with this herself, she finally broke down and declared to her mentor that she did not want to teach any more. After a lengthy conversation with her mentor, Naima finally shared her discomfort with some of the boys, and the one boy in particular.

Naima's program-based mentor immediately called a meeting with the school's assistant principal and the cooperating teacher. It turns out that the school was struggling with its "climate" of "sexual harassment," and Naima had picked up on and become a target in that climate. Her program-based mentor requested that the assistant principal and the cooperating teacher pursue a solution regarding the boy in question. The assistant principal did follow up, and the boy's behavior stopped. Naima never felt totally comfortable in her fourth period classroom, but she was able to teach.

Thanks to Naima, her program-based mentor and school representatives met with the college's Title IX coordinator and other experts to collaborate on working toward solving the school's climate of harassment. In the meantime, after her first placement, Naima was moved to another school where she felt more comfortable.

This story illustrates the importance of communicating with your program-based mentor, even if the subject makes you uncomfortable. That is what your mentor is there for. One wonders what might have happened to Naima's dream of being a high school teacher if she had kept her discomfort to herself. Samuel's story elaborates on this idea.

Samuel's Story

Samuel was assigned to a new school in a physical education class. He brought his student teaching handbook and his edTPA handbook with him on the first day to share with his cooperating teacher. The teacher told him that he had been teaching physical education for many years and did not believe in lesson plans, instruction, or assessments. Instead he felt his job was to just let kids play, and he would offer no instruction because that would inhibit their love of physical education.

Samuel figured that he could complete his lesson plans on his own and not mention it to anyone. However, after one week of standing with his back against the wall supervising students who were making mistakes when executing skills, while his cooperating teacher sat in his office, Samuel got worried. He knew that he would never learn to teach or meet his seminar requirements in this environment. He finally told his program-based mentor, who visited the next day. During the visit, his mentor was also told by the cooperating teacher that he did not believe in providing direct instruction in physical education.

Samuel's program-based mentor placed him in a new gym within a couple of days. Samuel lost some time that first week, but he was able to make up the time in his new placement, and he was able to instruct and assess students, prepare his edTPA videos, and make progress toward being the kind of physical education teacher he wanted to be. If Samuel had not communicated with his program-based mentor, he might not have been able to meet his course requirements or successfully prepare to teach.

Both narratives have in common the fact that the student teachers, despite the teacher preparation program clearly communicating with school administration, experienced problems once they got into the classroom. These were problems that required additional actions, beyond what the student teacher could handle alone.

These candidates needed help, and once they communicated this with their program-based mentors, they received help. Trust your instincts. If something about your placement seems wrong, speak up, and do not hesitate. If you feel that you are in a bad situation, it will likely not improve without some intervention.

YOUR PROGRAM-BASED MENTOR WILL HELP YOU BECOME AN EFFECTIVE TEACHER

Program-based mentors are sometimes education professors in a college program, but often they are adjuncts who are former school teachers or administrators, possessing deep knowledge about teaching and how schools work. The person in this role will provide you with invaluable expertise and support.

Your Mentor Will Evaluate Your Teaching

At multiple points during student teaching, your mentor will visit your classroom to observe your teaching. Program-based mentors are quite diverse. Some will be very strict about scheduling your observations well in advance and not deviating from the schedule; some will be more laid back and won't mind if an observation needs to be rescheduled. Some will hold you to very high expectations and evaluate you harshly, and some will compliment you and provide you with As. (Not easy As, because there is nothing easy about student teaching.)

Regardless of your program-based mentor's personality, you must communicate with them regularly, ensure that you are very clear about their expectations, and meet your commitments to them.

Plan to Communicate Frequently with Your Mentor

Ensure that you exchange phone and email information and keep in touch regularly with your mentor. Your program-based mentor may want to keep in touch with you via text rather than email, so ask them about their preferences, and if they attempt to contact you, make sure you get back to them right away. Do not let more than twelve hours go by without responding.

Also, ask your program-based mentor about hours when you can call or text. Some program-based mentors will not want to be disturbed after, say, 8:00 PM, and you do not want to irritate your clinical program-based mentor with what they consider a late-night call.

HOW DO OBSERVATIONS WORK?

Your program-based mentor will likely be the one who directs the observation schedule, so he or she will let you know days and times that work best for your observations. Sometimes the program-based mentor communicates directly with your cooperating teacher to schedule observations, but in most cases, you will be the go-between, so you need to be on top of it.

Make sure that you communicate with your cooperating teacher about a visit as soon as the day/time is offered by the program-based mentor. There may be a school event, such as an assembly or a field trip scheduled for that day, and you may not know about that yet.

Sometimes a schedule will have to change on either end, so it will likely be your job to negotiate that as well. You might ask your program-based mentor for a few days/times during a particular week and then have your cooperating teacher let you know what works best. Just be proactive about scheduling. Nothing irritates a mentor more than not getting a fast answer about when they can visit you. If your cooperating teacher is stalling or holding back the scheduling, let you program-based mentor know what's happening, but don't just silently wait. It will look like you are being negligent.

Also, it is very important that your observations include some sort of three-way debrief. This can be very challenging to schedule, so ask your cooperating teacher for help. Sometimes the school day is rushed and there is no free time when the teacher and program-based mentor can meet together with you. However, if you can schedule your observations around recess (when your cooperating teacher doesn't have duty) or a prep period, that will be helpful. You want to make sure that everyone is on the same page regarding your progress, so try to get everyone in the same room together.

Once you have scheduled your observation, you will send your lesson plan to your program-based mentor for feedback. Ask them to review your plan and offer suggestions for transitions, grouping students, differentiation, and also ask them to take a close look at the questions you plan to ask your students. Get some feedback on your planned questions to ensure that they are clear and that you are asking what you think you are asking.

Submitting your lesson plans before an observation is important because, if you do, your program-based mentor will have the opportunity to provide you with feedback on what plans need fine-tuning and/or revision so that your lesson goes smoothly and you demonstrate the criteria they are looking for. Even if your program does not require a lesson plan review prior to your observation, ask for one.

What Is Your Mentor Looking for When They Observe Your Teaching?

What is the program-based mentor looking for when they observe a lesson? You will likely be provided with an observation rubric from one of your mentors. This is the assessment tool that your program-based mentor will use to evaluate your lesson. The following are three important and common topics that your program-based mentor will be looking for and on which they will evaluate you:

Classroom Environment

- Do you demonstrate a good rapport (you get along) with your students?
- Are they respectful of you, and are you respectful of them?
- Do you encourage them to be respectful of each other?
- Do you manage transitions well?
- Do you implement class rules and routines?
- Do you monitor all of the students in the room?
- Do you effectively use age-appropriate classroom management techniques with your students?
- Are students engaged and attentive?
- Do you call on most of the students or just a few students?
- Do you provide structure by implementing procedures?

Instruction

- Do you manage time well?
- Do you demonstrate strong content knowledge (not making mistakes)?
- Do you ask challenging discussion questions and help students build on each other's responses?
- Can you lead a discussion?
- Are your explanations clear?
- Are you using age-appropriate vocabulary with your students?
- Are you using and supporting students to learn academic language?
- Do you differentiate for the students in your classroom?
- Are you aligning your instruction with students' prior knowledge and interests?
- Do you use space effectively?
- Do you make the learning accessible to all students?
- Do you seem comfortable teaching?
- Are you constantly assessing student learning?
- Can you make informal assessments and then change your instruction as needed?

Professionalism

- Do you communicate regularly with your program-based mentor?
- Do you respond promptly to your program-based mentor's questions and requests?
- Do you take critique well and attempt to apply your program-based mentor's suggestions?
- Are you prepared?
- Do you dress professionally?

TAKE AND APPLY YOUR PROGRAM-BASED MENTOR'S ADVICE

You must take their advice about your teaching and apply it. If your program-based mentor tells you to work on transitioning students from one activity to another, take their advice and suggestions and apply them. Work hard on transitions, and communicate with your program-based mentor about the strategies you are employing, and whether or not they are working.

It is a very good idea to communicate with your program-based mentor between observations also, sharing what you are attempting and how you think it is going, so that they know you are working hard to implement their suggestions.

And if their suggestions don't seem to be working, communicate that to them. Your program-based mentor is a professional who will know what to do. This individual will have numerous strategies in their "toolbox" for you to try.

Just don't make the mistake of not asking for help if you feel that you need it. If you feel shy about asking for help or worried that you are bugging them, you will have to push past this concern because it is not legitimate. Your mentor wants to help you.

You certainly don't want your program-based mentor to show up for an observation and see you struggling in the same manner that you were before, if you have had no communication in the interim. Your job, when you are struggling, is to communicate with your program-based mentor so that you can shift your challenges as an individual to a challenge that both of you are working hard to address together. When someone invests an effort into supporting you, they want you to succeed.

The Value of Reflection on Your Program-Based Mentor's Advice

Take the time to reflect on your program-based mentor's advice. Most programs have formalized this process so you will be asked to write a reflection after your observation and debrief, and you will likely have preassigned topics. Consider this reflection crucial, because it will provide you the opportunity to identify what you did well and how you did that, where you need to improve, and what steps you can take to improve.

Your reflections should include specific plans about how you will implement your program-based mentor's suggestions, and in the process of writing your reflections, you will likely discover questions you have about these topics that you can pursue with your program-based mentor.

To support your reflections on your lesson observation, below are some questions to consider based on the feedback you receive from your program-based mentor:

- If I could do the lesson over, what would I do the same, and what would I change?
- What are two criteria that I should focus on for improvement?
- What specific suggestions did I get from my program-based mentor about how to improve?
- What are two criteria with which I am doing well? How can I make certain that I continue this?
- Do my cooperating teacher and my program-based mentor agree on what I am doing well or where I need to improve? Where do they agree? Where do they disagree?
- How did I feel emotionally before my observation? What did I feel confident about and what did I feel nervous about? What can I do to feel less nervous and more prepared?
- Did anything my program-based mentor told me surprise me? If so, how can I follow up with them about that?
- Did I disagree with anything my program-based mentor said? How can I follow up about that?
- Who else might have a perspective on my lesson? How might my students or parents/guardians think about my observation lesson?
- Is there an educational researcher or theorist I have studied who would approve of my teaching methods or disapprove?

What Might Trip You Up When Being Observed, and How Can Your Program-Based Mentor Help?

The following narrative describes a student teacher who struggled with some *very common* challenges and was supported by her program-based mentor to overcome them.

Kim's Story

Kim was student teaching in a seventh grade school social studies classroom. On the day her program-based mentor came to observe her, she was teaching the students how to ask questions in order to analyze a primary source document.

Kim presented a mini-lesson to the students, and this went well. Kim modeled how to use a set of questions to analyze a primary source document, and then she engaged the students by asking them to help her examine the document and answer the questions. Kim used a graphic organizer presented on the SMART Board to illustrate this work. Kim asked several challenging discussion questions, and her students seemed on-task, engaged, and learning.

When she transitioned to the *independent practice* section in her lesson, however, the class began going downhill. Kim had planned to divide her class into groups of three, providing each group with its own primary source to analyze by applying the same question set to the new source, just as the class had done in the mini-lesson.

To transition from the mini-lesson, Kim first told the students to work in groups of three. She let her students choose their partners since, she told them, they had done "such a good job paying attention" during her mini-lesson. As soon as she did that, her program-based mentor observed students communicating in whispers or gestures about who would be in what group. Then the students started moving into their groups and the room became chaotic. Friends started talking and laughing while Kim focused on moving students without a group together into groups.

Then it was difficult to settle the class down. They were off-topic and socializing. Kim tried to provide the group instructions for the task, but the students were talking over her. She told the class to be quiet but proceeded to give the instructions even though several students were still talking.

Next, Kim proceeded to distribute the sources and the questions to the groups. While she was walking around distributing materials, a group of students started asking questions about what they were supposed to do because they were confused. Kim stopped at the group and spent several minutes working with the group to get them started, but she still had not passed out all of the materials and did not seem to be paying attention to the rest of the class. In fact, her back was turned to most of the class. A couple of students walked out of the room without asking permission.

The lesson described above may seem like an extreme situation, but Kim's teaching demonstrates some common scenarios described by program-based mentors. Kim's mentor had previously complimented Kim on her lesson plan and choice of materials, but was concerned about how quickly what had been an orderly classroom devolved into chaos.

Kim's program-based mentor noted that though Kim had written a strong plan, her challenge occurred when she sought to *implement* her lesson plan. For starters, even though the mini-lesson seemed to go well and some of the students demonstrated understanding, Kim had no plan to confirm that, once students moved into groups, they would be able to apply their learning to a new document without any review of the instructions.

Another error made by Kim was that she moved the students into groups before providing them with instructions. Once they became focused on the social dynamics involved in the groupings, they lost their interest and focus on the lesson. Though there may be appropriate times to let students choose their own groups, *placing the students in groups is more productive*. It resolves the anxiety that students feel about finding a group or connecting with friends, which is one reason why Kim's class became chaotic.

Finally, pausing to help a group before making sure that every student was clear about the directions was an error because students who were waiting to get started had nothing to do. Waiting for the teacher to provide them with materials, instructions, and support makes students feel frustrated and rebellious, or they simply focus on socializing, which makes the classroom chaotic. If students are not crystal clear about how to proceed, they will fill their time, and their choices are not always conducive to learning. The fact that Kim had her back turned to the majority of the class while helping one group prevented her from monitoring the whole class.

So her program-based mentor offered Kim the following tips that you will also find useful:

1. After introducing and practicing a skill or procedure, use a formative assessment to gauge the extent to which students understand and are ready to move on independently.
2. Provide clear instructions for the next activity and materials to the whole class. Review the instructions with the whole group and address any questions that students may have prior to moving them into groups. Ask students to repeat the instructions.
3. Assign students to random or prearranged groups.
4. Tell students that you will address their questions *three minutes after* they attempt to work independently. That will encourage them to try the activity rather than waiting for the teacher, and that will help them refine their questions as well.
5. Circulate through the room to ensure that everyone is clear and set up, and if you need to provide extra support to a group, do so while constantly looking up to monitor the class. Try not to spend more than two minutes with one group when you are circulating to ensure that everyone is getting started.

6. Though a teacher can never fully anticipate what might prove confusing or difficult for students, if you differentiate the work you assign each group by putting the appropriate supports and challenges in place prior to instruction, the independent work will go more smoothly. If your advanced students have appropriate challenges that will engage them and if your struggling students have the necessary supports to help them accomplish the activity, they will be able to meet with success.

If Kim had anticipated that the directions might be unclear for a particular group, she could have provided a clear example on the paper as a model to get them started. It is never enough to just have a general plan to circulate through the class and observe how students are doing, fine-tuning and supporting them as needed. It is important to anticipate where they will struggle or need more challenge before teaching the lesson.

Dolores's Story

The following narrative illustrates a less-common challenge for student teachers, but it will provide additional insight into how your program-based mentor might support you.

Dolores was a student teaching candidate who got a slow start. She was placed in a general elementary classroom, but told the cooperating teacher that she was only comfortable working with small groups. Dolores stated that she really wanted to be a teacher, but she felt uncomfortable with the fifth grade class she was assigned to. She wanted to teach elementary but not that level. So she spent her first week responding to student work and working with one small group of students. By her second week, when her program-based mentor contacted her to check in and schedule her first observation, she told her program-based mentor that everything was going well.

When the program-based mentor contacted the cooperating teacher, she told the program-based mentor that she was concerned about Dolores and wasn't sure she had "what it takes" to teach. The cooperating teacher described Dolores as very hesitant to work with the students, preferring to sit at the teacher's desk and review student work, work on her lesson plans, or work with individuals or one small group.

So the program-based mentor and Dolores had a candid conversation. Dolores assured her program-based mentor that she really did want to be a teacher, but she felt intimidated by the students and just was not ready. The program-based mentor pushed Dolores and told her that she needed to teach a lesson to the whole class by the end of the third week. Dolores felt terrified, but she did teach an ELA (her major) lesson on poetry to the class, and both she and the cooperating teacher reported that the class "went well."

The program-based mentor then scheduled her first formal observation for the following week. When she came to observe, Dolores delivered the lesson but her demeanor "seemed flat." She did not smile or interact with the students very much. When the program-based mentor asked her why, Dolores stated that she just felt too nervous to do more then get through the lesson she had planned.

The program-based mentor advised Dolores to rehearse her lesson plan prior to implementing it so that she could focus less on what she had to do next and more on the students and their learning as well as her interactions with them. If Dolores felt confident about her plan, she might relax a bit and then focus on teaching. Dolores followed this advice, and the next lesson went a little better. Every time Dolores delivered a lesson, her confidence grew, and soon she began smiling and interacting with her students. Still, though, she was not comfortable enough to demonstrate that she could run her own class and veer from her plan if students needed extra instruction or an alternative approach.

So after conversing, Dolores and her program-based mentor concluded that though she was making progress, she needed more time practicing. Together with other program personnel, they decided to add an additional semester to Dolores's course of studies. This was unfortunate because Dolores had been eager to graduate and start teaching, but in the long run, her program-based mentor convinced her that she simply needed more practice in order to become an educator who felt confident and comfortable. She needed extra time. And now Dolores is a tenured teacher happily working in a school.

Having honest conversations with your program-based mentor will be helpful to you, and so will demonstrating that you will do whatever it takes to prepare for the job of teaching. One lesson in Dolores's case was that even though she struggled, Dolores was told that if she really wanted to be a teacher, she would have to work a bit harder and longer to get there. Demonstrating to her mentor that she was willing to work hard to make progress helped get them on her side and encouraged them to support Dolores to achieve her dream.

REFLECTING ON THE CHAPTER

In this chapter you learned about your program-based mentor, how he/she/they will support you, and what they will expect from you. You also read some narratives about student teachers and their experiences in order to provide you with specific illustrations of issues that may come up in your own student teaching.

To reflect on your reading, consider writing a list of questions you may have for your program-based mentor about what their expectations will be for you and how you can expect them to support you.

Also, write some reminders about how you will attempt to maintain proactive communication with your mentors.

Chapter Three

Working with Key School Stakeholders

As soon as you begin student teaching, your primary focus in life will likely center on what is happening in your classroom. Your interactions and relationships with students and school personnel, as well as your responsibilities in your classroom and school, will take on tremendous importance for you. One reason for that is because schools are incredibly busy places. The demands made on your time and attention are usually immediate, and you will have strong emotions about what happens in your classroom and with your students, especially during student teaching.

On some days you will feel successful and you will float on air for the rest of the day, and other days will not go as planned and you will feel disappointed and uncertain. The unpredictability of classroom life is exciting and emotional because one can never completely anticipate what will happen in a classroom on any given day.

So in the midst of the emotions, the demands, and the chaos of a student teaching life, take time to deliberately build positive relationships with the people you interact with at school every day, especially your students, and intentionally reflect on what you learn from these individuals about how to forge positive and productive relationships. That way you can use your student teaching experiences to develop the skills—the blueprints—you will need to foster the kinds of relationships that will support you throughout your teaching life.

The advice in this chapter will support those efforts by discussing ways to work effectively with key school personnel, students, and their parents/guardians.

YOUR COOPERATING TEACHER

The relationship you build with your cooperating teacher will be significant and will likely have an impact on your early teaching career, so most of this chapter is devoted to that individual.

The cooperating teacher is the teacher with whom you will work every day when student teaching. This person will be the primary mentor who provides you with resources, works with you to lay out your teaching and assignment schedule, helps record your lessons for the edTPA or a class assignment, communicates with personnel in your teacher preparation program, and completes evaluations on your behalf. In many programs, the cooperating teacher will be asked to assign you a grade for your student teaching.

Your cooperating teacher is the one who has taken on the vast responsibility for your development during student teaching and for launching you into the profession. This individual will function as both your partner in the classroom, with whom you will create wonderful moments for your students, and your immediate supervisor.

By the time you begin student teaching, you will have learned a great deal from your professors and other mentors in your teacher preparation program. However, it can be argued that you will learn as much or more from your cooperating teacher, who will be showing you the ropes, showing you how classroom teaching really works, and will be the one preparing you and giving you the opportunities you need to be ready to teach.

Consider Kathy's story, which illustrates just a fraction of what you can learn from your cooperating teacher:

Kathy's Story

Kathy was excited to learn that she would be student teaching seventh and eighth grade math during the spring semester in a large, urban school. But as Kathy walked through the halls with her administrator to her classroom on the first day, her stomach was in knots and she grew increasingly anxious. There were so many students, some of them were bigger than she was, and they seemed loud and unruly in the school hallways. Kathy had never felt intimidated by middle school students before, such as during her field observations, but now the prospect of being their teacher made the endeavor seem daunting.

Kathy felt confident about her subject matter, but was not sure she could lead these loud, large students. On the first day, Kathy sat off to the side and observed. She watched her cooperating teacher, Ms. Nichols, stand outside the classroom door and greet each student by name as they came in the room. The students entered the classroom and sat in their preassigned groups. When the bell rang, Ms. Nichols closed the door. Kathy noticed that if a student was late, they were not permitted to enter unless Ms. Nichols went to the door to let them in.

Then, to Kathy's amazement, Ms. Nichols directed the students to put their feet on the floor and close their eyes. With a small gong, she led them in a two-minute meditation. Kathy witnessed every student participate easily in the ritual. Then, without missing a beat, Ms. Nichols began the class with a "Do Now."

Throughout the lesson, as Ms. Nichols introduced math topics, she invited students to make connections between their lives and the topic at hand. They discussed family members and after-school jobs. The students seemed comfortable and engaged. And when it was time to take the calculators from the closet, two students quietly distributed them while the class listened to directions.

When it was time for students to write or work independently, another student got up and turned on classical music. When students were assigned group work, each one was given a specific task, such as notetaker, timekeeper, presenter, and manager.

Kathy also noticed that the students had created beautiful posters displayed on the back wall related to math topics.

When conducting her initial observations of her student teaching classroom, Kathy learned that Ms. Nichols was inviting and supportive, but also she had clearly set up a structured environment in which her students knew what to do in terms of transitions and class routines. The students were always clear about what to do, and they were consistently focused and busy.

Working in Ms. Nichols's room certainly made Kathy's transition from observer to student teacher go smoothly, because Ms. Nichols had set up consistent procedures and had established strong relationships with her students by consistently inviting them to bring their interests into the math work. Kathy could implement the structures that had already been established and spend her time discussing the topics with her students, getting to know them, and teaching them rather than disciplining or "controlling" them, which had been the source of her initial intimidation.

When Kathy was invited to join the staff as a new math teacher the following year, she continued to implement the procedures Ms. Nichols had taught her.

In Kathy's case, she entered a classroom that had been up and running for several months, and though she was not able to observe Ms. Nichols teach the procedures and routines to the class, Kathy was able to observe and implement them. Kathy had learned about classroom management in her program-based methods courses, but it wasn't until she encountered strong, structured methods that were implemented in a real classroom that she was able to connect her previous learning to student teaching. Kathy was fortunate to have a strong model of how to create a structured, inviting teaching and learning environment.

So what can you expect to learn from your cooperating teacher, and how will they support your development?

Here is a list of the ways in which your cooperating teacher will help you:

- Your cooperating teacher will share the classroom curriculum and other curricular resources with you.
- Your cooperating teacher will provide you with the lesson plan that they use to organize their lessons.
- Your cooperating teacher will influence when and how you interact with students, scheduling your progress from observing, to working with individuals and small groups, to teaching the entire class.
- Your cooperating teacher will show you how classroom resources are organized and allocated.
- Your cooperating teacher will demonstrate how he or she uses a variety of classroom technologies such as class Dojo and the SMART Board.
- Your cooperating teacher will demonstrate effective classroom management strategies.
- Your cooperating teacher will invite you to after-school meetings and/or other PD (professional development) opportunities, such as conferences.
- Your cooperating teacher will introduce you to key school personnel.
- Your cooperating teacher will model for you how to communicate with parents and other stakeholders.
- Your cooperating teacher will demonstrate how and when to implement a variety of assessments.
- Your cooperating teacher will demonstrate and give you practice differentiation instruction.
- Your cooperating teacher will demonstrate how to effectively group and manage groups of students.
- You cooperating teacher will demonstrate how to deal with disciplinary issues or classroom bullying.
- Your cooperating teacher will demonstrate how to give feedback to students and how to help students use feedback.
- Your cooperating teacher will demonstrate how to transition students from one activity to another.
- Your cooperating teacher will examine your written lesson plans and give you feedback.

- Your cooperating teacher will observe you when you teach and provide you with honest, low-stakes, and frequent feedback.
- Your cooperating teacher will be your advocate when you struggle.
- Your cooperating teacher will support your efforts to secure video release forms and record your teaching.
- Your cooperating teacher will introduce you to other responsibilities (non-teaching) that teachers fill their days with.
- Your cooperating teacher will assign a grade to characterize your student teaching placement.

Given all of this (and more), it is easy to understand the importance of that professional relationship, and how necessary it will be to foster and maintain a positive working relationship with this individual. It is quite possible that you and your cooperating teacher will naturally have good chemistry and much in common, and you will get along quite well. It is also possible that your cooperating teacher is quite different from you, and you wouldn't necessarily be friends outside of the school. Either way, none of that matters. You must work hard to build and maintain a positive working relationship with this mentor.

How do you go about doing that? First and foremost, if you always consider your cooperating teacher your supervisor or "boss," that will help you keep in mind how crucial this person is to your success. When you student teach, your supervisor is a cooperating teacher. Next year, your supervisor will be your assistant principal or principal. Learning how to manage a relationship with your immediate supervisor is crucial, and it is up to you. Your cooperating teacher (future principal) does not need you as much as you need them, so the bulk of the responsibility in the relationship falls on you.

And even if you feel that your cooperating teacher (future principal) is overly demanding, uncooperative, unclear, or too busy to give you everything you need at times, you still must work hard to maintain a positive relationship with them. This is a skill set that you will need to develop in student teaching, if you have not done so before, and carry it with you through your entire career. When interacting with your cooperating teacher or any supervisor, strive to be proactive, positive, and professional.

Proactive

From the moment you walk into your school, strive to be proactive. You want to take advantage of every learning opportunity that will be offered to you and seek out opportunities when you find them. Again, your cooperating teacher will be extremely busy. All teachers are. You must not add to their burden by being so passive that they have to spend time inventing things for you to do. And remember that proactive people don't just do what is expected of them; being proactive means that you seek out ways to go above and beyond what is expected of you. Make yourself *indispensable*.

If the teacher puts students in groups, ask if you can jump in during your first few days and work with a group. If the teacher is preparing materials, offer to help. Offer to organize bookshelves and help put work on the walls or create bulletin boards. If the cooperating teacher must attend professional development meetings on Monday afternoons, ask if you can also sit in and participate. If copies need to be made, offer to make them. And if you have helpful and relevant resources that you have located on your own or that you have been given in a teacher education class, share them.

Many cooperating teachers appreciate learning some of the cutting-edge educational practices and theories that you are learning and will find these resources helpful. If you are good with technology and know of educational software and apps that your cooperating teacher is not using, offer to show the cooperating teacher how to use them.

Be very clear about what you are supposed to do so that you will be not just proactive but also effective. If you are proactive, your cooperating teacher will certainly appreciate you and praise you to other school personnel. This will help you earn recommendations and maybe even a job in the school.

In addition, make sure that you are proactive about your needs in terms of class assignments or your edTPA preparations. Show your cooperating teacher your seminar schedule and describe the kinds of activities you are expected to engage in (such as designing lesson plans you can teach and assessing them) as well as the progression you are expected to follow (such as moving from working with small groups to teaching all day).

You will also need to remind your cooperating teacher to fill out your evaluations and facilitate that by providing them with an envelope or the link to your program's evaluation program. Even if your program has already communicated this to your cooperating teacher, he or she is very busy and will need reminders from you, and it is your responsibility to ask them to help you accomplish your college requirements.

Positive

Be friendly. Be appreciative and say "thank you." When you receive a critique, try not to react to it as if it is a criticism. View critiques as advice to act on—an opportunity to grow. Approach any work that is given to you, such as lesson planning, supervision (as long as you are never left in a classroom alone), assessment, or the organization of materials as an opportunity to learn how to complete those tasks, because a teacher's day is not just delivering lessons. Supervisory duties, bulletin boards, meetings, grading, and organizing materials are also a big part of the job.

Even if your cooperating teacher isn't particularly friendly, push yourself to be so. Smile and say "thank you." And remember, there will be days when, for one reason or another, your cooperating teacher disappoints or upsets you. If this happens and it is significant enough to discuss with them, do so in an appreciative way, using "I" messages, and never accuse your cooperating teacher of negative thoughts or actions. There will also be days when you are feeling like you are doing such a good job, any critique seems unnecessary. But take the critique anyhow, and remember that it is your cooperating teacher's responsibility to give it to you. No teacher is ever perfect; that is why the job is so fun and challenging.

There will also be times when you question or disagree with your cooperating teacher's approach. When this happens, feel free to question their decisions in a positive way by asking, "I was wondering why you did . . . or said," but always from the point of view that you are trying to learn from them, not evaluate them. It is never a good idea to challenge your cooperating teacher and make them feel defensive. And of course, even if you are feeling upset with your cooperating teacher, make sure that you never ever take out your frustration on your students. In fact, if you direct your focus away from your cooperating teacher and toward your wonderful students in a moment of frustration, you will likely feel better.

Professional

Your cooperating teacher is sacrificing valuable class time with his or her students in order to "pay it forward," supporting both your development as a highly skilled educator and your future students. That is no small thing. You should know that cooperating teachers receive very little in exchange for their efforts, so make their sacrifice of time worth it by giving them your all.

Always be on time. Nothing makes a cooperating teacher more frustrated than student teachers who do not show up to school on time. And always be prepared. If the cooperating teacher asks you to plan a lesson for the next day, make sure that you get that done. And if you are not certain how to go about making the plan, always ask questions. Do not just assume that you will figure out what you need to know in order to complete any duty assigned to you. If you mess up because you did not ask, that will impact the cooperating teacher's busy schedule and the students as well.

Always act professionally as well. Even if you feel that your cooperating teacher and you have a wonderful relationship and are very friendly, do not assume that you are friends. Do not share personal information with your cooperating teacher that could make you seem immature or unreliable, such as a wild weekend or maxing out a credit card. Keep your personal life to yourself, outside of the normal topics that professionals share with each other. And respect your cooperating teacher's time. Even if she or he seems sympathetic to challenges you have in your personal life, they did not sign up to be your personal therapist, and no matter how nice they are, they may eventually resent taking time away from serving their students to listen to your problems. Don't ask for special favors, don't ask your cooperating teacher if you can leave early, and keep your phone put away when you are working.

If you get frustrated or upset about something that your cooperating teacher says or does, handle it with the utmost professionalism. Do not yell at them or accuse them of sabotaging you. If you need to discuss something that has impacted you in a negative way, do so professionally and calmly. And do rely on your college-based mentors to help you figure out how to broach uncomfortable subjects in a professional manner, or even to take over the conversation in a three-way meeting. Your college mentors have a lot of experience with this, and it is their job to advocate for you. So rather than handling an emotional or upsetting conversation on your own, seek help if you need it.

Consider John's story as an example of how important it is to maintain professionalism and positivity in order to sustain a positive relationship with your cooperating teacher while student teaching.

John's Story

John was a secondary ELA candidate who was assigned to student teach in a large, competitive suburban high school. His cooperating teacher, Ms. Madison, was a veteran teacher at the school and also the English department chair, and she taught the honors and AP sections of English in her high school. Ms. Madison asked John to interview with her prior to accepting him as a student teacher.

In the interview they discussed books that John hoped to teach someday, and he was asked about the qualities he felt he possessed that would make him a good student teacher. John described himself as an excellent student and told Ms. Madison about his experience tutoring secondary students while in college.

Ms. Madison accepted John as a student teacher, and he started working with her on the first day of school. John was proactive. He read all of the assigned books prior to the semester, shared ideas he had for learning activities in the class, wrote lesson plans that Ms. Madison checked, and started teaching the whole group by the second week of school. When his program-based mentor came for his first observation, his supervisor told him that he was doing very well and he gave him some pointers to fine-tune his teaching. For example, his supervisor instructed John to focus on the questions he posed to students prior to teaching, and suggested revising his questions so that they would be precise and generate the kinds of discussions John was hoping for.

Ms. Madison observed John frequently and provided him with feedback. Sometimes the feedback surprised him. For example, Ms. Madison made John aware of the fact that he was almost exclusively calling on the boys who sat to his left and would aggressively raise their hands, ignoring the girls to his right, who often had the correct responses but were more hesitant to share. In addition to being more mindful about calling on more students, Ms. Madison also recommended a seating chart to mix the students up and some teaching strategies that would invite more students to participate in class discussions.

When it came time for John to read and respond to student work, he was shocked at how long it took him to review student papers. In the beginning he was spending almost an hour on each student. When he asked Ms. Madison for support, she provided him with a word bank of comments that he could reference when responding to student work. Not having to come up with original feedback for similar strengths and weaknesses in student papers did indeed enable John to work more quickly.

As John neared the end of his placement, he grew frustrated and confined by the guidance Ms. Madison was providing him. She would sit at the back of the room, take notes, and then, *in his view*, share everything he had done wrong with him. He began to feel as if she were nitpicky and overly critical when, from his perspective, he could have taken over her schedule and been the real classroom teacher at any moment. John got to a point where he didn't want any more feedback. He just wanted to teach, unencumbered.

John did not know how to approach Ms. Madison about this issue, so he never said anything, but he did vent to the other English teachers in the school, younger teachers with whom he felt friendly. And when he did, John presented Ms. Madison as overly critical and unsupportive. He even suspected that she was a little jealous of his teaching talents.

The other teachers told Ms. Madison about some of John's concerns. Ms. Madison was shocked, but she did not confront John. Instead, they finished the semester, she gave him a party, and took him out to dinner to celebrate the end of his placement.

It was over dinner that Ms. Madison recommended to John that in the future, in professional situations, he should voice his concerns directly to his colleagues or supervisor, rather than vent behind their backs. She let him know that she wasn't hurt and that she would certainly write him a strong recommendation, but she also wanted him to know that she had been told about his frustration with her, all the while never seeing any indication of frustration from him.

John graduated and started teaching in an urban high school with a challenging population. It was only then that he realized that the comments he had received from Ms. Madison were not criticism but feedback to help him when he was working with more challenging students. He was happy that he had saved her notes and was able to apply her suggestions to his new context.

In John's case, he was lucky. Ms. Madison was an experienced cooperating teacher who dealt with her knowledge that John was talking behind her back to her colleagues with maturity and patience. Another cooperating teacher may not have been so professional and supportive, so this story serves as a reminder to communicate positively and professionally with your cooperating teacher first when you feel there is a problem, and then with your program-based mentor if the problem does not get resolved or you do not have a better understanding of the situation. Do not engage in negative social behaviors at school.

In addition to working closely with your cooperating teacher, you will likely have the opportunity to interact with a variety of school personnel. In the spirit of being proactive, strive to gain an understanding of who works in the school and what they do. This will further educate you about how schools function, and also enable you to ask school personnel for help when you need it. This is an important habit to get into for your future teaching. In addition, because there are many jobs in a school, each person can offer you advice and perspective on the profession of teaching.

ADMINISTRATION

The school administrator who will supervise you is likely the school's principal or assistant principal. This is the person to whom you will report on your first day of student teaching, the person who has likely agreed to take you on as a student teacher, and the person who will have likely assigned you to your cooperating teacher.

As directed by your student teaching seminar instructor, you will contact and/or meet either your school principal or assistant principal on the first day that you start working at the school. This administrator is likely the person who has coordinated your student teaching experience with your program. On your first day, this administrator will welcome you, ask you some questions about yourself, and introduce you to your cooperating teacher, if you have not met them previously.

The administrator might give you a tour of the school and share contextual information about the school and community. Feel free to take notes while you meet with them, as you will likely be asked to describe your student teaching context, perhaps as a class assignment and certainly on the edTPA.

Some administrators are very hands-off, while others will ask you to submit your lesson plans for their feedback and might even sit in to watch you teach at some point during your placement. If this idea makes you feel nervous, don't worry—you are not alone. But if an administrator is willing to take the time to mentor you in any way, it is because they are invested, like your mentors, in helping you develop into the best teacher you can be. And your mentors will assure you that even experienced teachers feel nervous when an administrator sits in.

Know that being observed is part of the job, do your best, and be appreciative of any feedback you receive. Like your mentors, no one expects you to be perfect; they just want to see effort and progress along the way. In some districts, if you want to substitute teach while you are looking for a permanent position, it is the school administrator who will nominate you. Also, your administrator may use his or her contacts to get you a job either in the school or in the district. At the very least, they will be able to provide a job reference for you, so demonstrate that you are proactive and embody positivity and professionalism at all times with this person.

OTHER SCHOOL PERSONNEL

In addition to interacting with your cooperating teacher and supervising administrator, it will be important for you to put yourself out there and build collegial relationships with other school personnel as well. These are the people with whom you will interact almost daily in your student teaching context and who will be very helpful to you as a student teacher (and teacher) in ways that you likely cannot imagine yet.

There is a range of school personnel with whom you will likely interact when student teaching. These people will be able to provide you with important information about all of the resources and supports available to students in your school, as well as the community/students/school. It is a good idea to make yourself familiar with their roles, if you are not already familiar with them. Again, you'll want to add the important task of getting to know school personnel into your blueprints.

Here is a list of school personnel you'll want to meet:

School counselor
Speech therapist
Occupational therapist
Physical therapist
Reading specialist
Intervention specialist
Athletic coach
Administrative assistant
School nutritionist/cook
Teacher's aide
Paraprofessional
Computer technician
Parent coordinator/community outreach
School nurse
Athletic coaches

Plan to take some time during your first week and introduce yourself to those who fill key jobs in a school, and consider asking these people the following questions when you introduce yourself to them:

- What is your primary job at this school?
- How specifically do you support teachers and students?
- Under what circumstances might I get in touch with you for support?
- What should I know about the community/school/students to be successful in this school?

Spotlight on the School's Administrative Assistant

For example, the school's administrative assistant is a crucial person to know because he or she has the "big picture" view of how the school works, can direct you to resources you will need, and will likely be the one who verifies your student teaching hours. In addition, the school secretary often has the ear of the school administrator and may put a good word in for you if a job becomes available at the school. When interacting with the school secretary, introduce yourself and always be friendly—not demanding.

Spotlight on the Parent Coordinator

If your school has a parent coordinator, this is an important person for you to know. The parent coordinator will be able to fill you in about the school community, the level of parent involvement and any challenges in this regard, and community resources as well. The parent coordinator will also be able to give you a sense of the various community resources that you might be able to leverage when working with students and communicating with parents.

Spotlight on the Librarian/Media Specialist

The school librarian/media specialist is also an important person to know. This individual will have myriad resources that they can make available to support your lesson planning. You will develop a positive relationship with this individual if you stop by their space—the library or media center—introduce yourself, and let them know some of the curricula you are working with. This individual will be able to recommend resources that are age-appropriate and streamlined, as well as reading materials that you can use to supplement your lesson plans. Media specialists love to support teachers, as long as they get enough notice so that they can fit you into their schedule.

OTHER TEACHERS IN THE SCHOOL

Naturally you will interact with other teachers in the school, and you will likely be introduced to them by your cooperating teacher. Getting to know other teachers will benefit you immensely. You will gain a sense of how they work with students in different subjects and at different grade levels, and they may be able to shed light on particular students you presently work with. The camaraderie that you may form with a group of teachers who have lunch together every day will help acclimate you to the school, make you feel supported, and help you gain a sense of the school and community culture.

Gossip

The teachers' lounge, where you will likely interact with other teachers, is a place where you can learn a great deal, but it can also contain obstacles. Be wary there, because sometimes there are school politics at work that you could inadvertently be drawn into, or you could find yourself involved in a nasty gossip session about administration that you do not want to get caught up in. When the social dynamic involving other teachers in the school goes sour for student teachers, that can be very challenging for them, so do tread lightly and know that with advance planning, you can avoid negative situations. Consider Sahara's story:

Sahara's Story

Sahara had been encouraged to be friendly and get to know the other teachers by her college student teaching seminar instructor, but she had simultaneously been warned not to participate in gossip and to politely excuse herself or change the subject when the teachers' conversations went in a negative direction. Though she found this situation difficult to navigate at some points, Sahara kept this in mind from the beginning of her student teaching experience.

When Sahara was in the lunchroom with her cooperating teacher and the teachers were informally planning or sharing stories about their families or weekends, she always participated in the conversations. She also sought advice from the other teachers in regard to lesson planning, assessments, and individual students. However, whenever the conversation turned to a subject that was negative—such as complaining about other teachers or administration, Sahara pretended that she had to prepare for the next class, make copies, complete a school assignment (during free time), etc., and made a graceful exit.

Because of Sahara's frequent and positive interactions with the group, the other teachers did not seem to mind or notice when she excused herself. But her administrator had somehow figured this out.

On her last day, the administrator pulled Sahara aside and told her that she was looking forward to writing her a recommendation and considering her for the next available teaching position in the school. The administrator praised Sahara's initiative and progress, and she specifically told Sahara that she also appreciated the fact that Sahara did not engage in school gossip. Sahara never really understood how her administrator knew that she had been determined to rise above the gossip, but somehow she did, and Sahara remembered that for the rest of her professional life.

PARENTS

You will certainly have the opportunity to interact with parents in some way while student teaching, and this is a great thing, because much of your teaching life will involve communicating with parents. If you student teach in the fall, you will observe how your cooperating teacher manages back-to-school night, when he or she introduces themselves (and you) to parents, and provides an overview of the curriculum, classroom resources, and expectations. Observe how your cooperating teacher addresses parent questions and concerns, and make a note of that, because your future parents will likely have similar questions and concerns.

Observe how your cooperating teacher navigates parent-teacher conferences. If possible, plan to sit in on all of these. You will learn a great deal about the school, the community, and the particular students in your class. Notice how the teacher both highlights what the student has done well and raises concerns about academic struggles or behavior. If the cooperating teacher recommends an evaluation, how do they handle that?

In addition, take note of how the cooperating teacher communicates with parents on a daily basis. Do they use an app in order to maintain a flow of communication? Do they send letters home frequently? Do they email? If a student is missing homework assignments or is not doing well on assessments, when and how does this get communicated? How does the cooperating teacher share good news with parents when a student does something particularly well? How does the teacher navigate tense conversations or difficult, confrontational parents?

Try to participate in as many parent-teacher interactions as possible, and reflect on what seems to work and what doesn't. Be cautious when interacting with parents, however, because sometimes parents try to communicate with student teachers in an attempt to get information about their student that should only come from the cooperating teacher, or they may try to get the student teacher in their corner if they are in a conflict with the classroom teacher. Don't ever promise to keep a conversation confidential or engage in a difficult conversation without your cooperating teacher present.

YOUR STUDENTS

Student teaching is a memorable experience, and though you may not stay in the same school where you student teach for your first job, you will always remember the people you worked with during student teaching, and this is especially true for your students. Sometimes students welcome student teachers with open arms. They are thrilled to have another teacher in the class, especially one who is new and excited, full of youthful energy. They will sense that from you and appreciate your enthusiasm.

Other times, it takes a bit longer to feel comfortable and welcomed by your students, especially if they are older and less inclined to show you how excited they are to have you there. But generally, by the time you leave your placement, you will have bonded with your students, or at least many of them. In many cases the student teacher's last day is a sad affair, especially in the elementary grades.

So how does an effective student teacher communicate with students in order to build positive and productive relationships with them? First, always remember why you are there—your main goal for being a teacher is likely that you want to serve the students. That is the most important thing. Sometimes you will support your students by assigning them challenging work or having a firm conversation, but as long as you remember that you are the leader, and you are there to provide them with your very best, they will pick up on that and work with you.

Throughout this book, methods for connecting curriculum, assessment, and instruction to students' prior learning and interests have been discussed, as has the idea of creating a positive learning environment in which you communicate respectfully and support students to do the same with you and each other. This book also highlights ways to be explicit about how you expect students to behave and manage time, routines, transitions, and materials. If students are clearly told what is expected of them, they will rise to your expectations. It is when the teacher is unclear, uncertain, or inconsistent that chaos ensues, and that can damage your relationship with your students.

Remain True to Yourself when Managing Your Students

Because you will be entering someone else's classroom, it is likely that your cooperating teacher has already implemented or will implement a toolbox full of classroom management techniques that they have refined over the years. Use your cooperating teacher as a model and try out their classroom management tools and techniques, but know that you don't have to function as a carbon copy of them. In your initial days in the classroom, you will observe your cooperating teacher and consider not only their classroom management strategies but also how they communicate with the students.

There is nothing wrong, when you begin working with students, with emulating your cooperating teacher's communication style as you get comfortable and find your voice. As you gain experience and confidence, you will keep some of what they do and add your own communication styles. Just remember, as you find your way—never make assumptions about students' motivations, check your biases, and always treat your students with the utmost respect. Do not vent about particular students with school personnel, because that actually makes things worse. You will better manage your class and motivate them to do their best if you work hard to get to know them, honor their effort and achievements, listen to them, appreciate their perspectives and interests, and always put their needs first.

Heidi's Story

Heidi was excited to start student teaching in a third grade, general education classroom. She had enjoyed working as a camp counselor and as an after-school tutor, and she had loved interacting with students during her field observation in her earlier education courses. Heidi was an easygoing, friendly person with a smile for everyone. However, when her program-based supervisor observed her, he noticed that Heidi seemed tense, strict, and even harsh with her students. Using intimidating, almost hostile language, she would say, "Stop talking. Right now." "Pay attention, because you don't know what you are doing." "What is your problem?"

Heidi as a student teacher did not resemble the Heidi that the supervisor had met during orientation or the Heidi he had observed during their check-ins. So the supervisor asked Heidi to describe how she went about creating a "positive classroom environment." This topic is a required edTPA topic, and the candidate must demonstrate in their video and commentary how they have established an environment in which they demonstrate "respect and rapport" with their students, challenging their students but also offering a "low risk" environment where students are not afraid to fail.[1]

Heidi asserted that she was challenging her students and that her cooperating teacher had warned her not to be "too soft" with the students. "Don't smile and don't be too nice, or they will take advantage of you," she was told. The cooperating teacher had even told Heidi about the old adage, "Don't smile until Christmas." So Heidi had assumed her cooperating teacher's personality and created a well-managed but very unfriendly atmosphere in her classroom.

The supervisor asked her if she enjoyed teaching in this environment and, at that moment, Heidi broke down. She described feeling more like a "prison warden" than a teacher and recalled her own favorite teachers, who had been warm and caring and interested in their students' lives. Those were the teachers who had inspired her to become one herself. The supervisor diplomatically followed up with the classroom teacher and Heidi, and both encouraged her to bring her own, unique personality into the classroom while using some of the classroom management techniques employed by the cooperating teacher.

The supervisor conveyed to Heidi that in his experience, forging supportive and warm, but always professional, relationships with students would help everyone in the class feel comfortable and would also motivate students to do well.

Heidi was soon herself again, interacting warmly with her students and growing increasingly more comfortable as a teacher. She began to enjoy the students, and they in turn, soon adored her, providing her not only with strong evidence of their learning and a positive classroom environment but also a beautiful thank-you card at the end of her placement.

The lesson here is: Don't ever let someone tell you that you have to be mean to students in order to successfully manage a classroom or act in a way that goes against your nature when dealing with the other people in your school.

REFLECTING ON THE CHAPTER

To reflect on this chapter, recall all of the people with whom you will be interacting in your school context. Rehearse in your mind how you want to present yourself. If someone was speaking about you and you weren't there, what would you hope they would say? How can you present yourself in a way that will accomplish that? Also, imagine the challenging situations that might present themselves and how you would like to handle them. That will help you rehearse for similar situations that may arise.

NOTE

1. Board of Trustees of the Leland Stanford Junior University (2018).

Preface to Chapters 4 and 5

Teachers work hard. Their day does not begin when they walk into the school, and it does not end when they leave. Teachers spend weekends, early mornings, and evenings preparing lessons and materials, responding to and evaluating student work, and communicating with students and families via email. Teachers devote hours of their lives to team meetings with their colleagues and engaged in professional development, even in the summer. As a result, trying to describe everything that a teacher must know and be able to do on any given day is virtually impossible. The work that teachers do is incredibly complex, and the knowledge that a teacher accumulates over time and with experience is vast.

The only way to really understand a teacher's life and get a sense of all they must know and be able to do is to work as a teacher. You will soon discover as you student teach that everything you have learned in your methods classes about instructional design is only a fraction of what teachers do every day. You will feel overwhelmed on occasion, but that does not mean you are not capable. Being overwhelmed sometimes is also part of the job. With strong mentoring, you will surely develop the knowledge and confidence to do this demanding job.

The next two chapters will support your efforts to design instructional plans (chapter 4) and their related assessments (chapter 5) that will support diverse learners and align with your disciplinary standards. The term "learning segment" will be used to describe a mini-unit that can be taught in about one week, usually consisting of three to five lesson plans. This term is used on the edTPA and many student teaching preparation programs. If you must take the edTPA for state certification, these chapters will support your edTPA preparations for Task 1.

Chapter Four

Designing High-Quality Lesson Plans

Design Your Lessons with Attention to the Details

With strong mentoring, the kind described in chapters 2 and 3, you will surely develop the knowledge and confidence to do the demanding job of being a teacher. In addition, as you learn to teach, pay close attention to all of the topics and the details (such as academic language and differentiated instruction) that you need to consider when designing lesson plans.

Learning how to address all of the topics that you have to keep in mind when planning a lesson will sometimes seem burdensome, and sometimes overly technical and uninspired. But try to push through that feeling and remember that student teaching is the time to start designing your blueprints and investing time in that technical work so that you can be inspired and creative.

If an architect attempts to build a structure on flimsy or incomplete plans, the time and materials will be wasted when the structure collapses. Extend this metaphor to the classroom. If a teacher prepares flimsy or incomplete plans, students lose the opportunity to learn.

By giving each lesson-planning topic the attention that it needs in your early days of learning to teach, you will soon develop the habit of addressing all of the topics, and, very soon, that work will feel less challenging because you will have developed the habit of considering each topic. When teachers come up with wonderful ideas for a lesson, it sometimes feels instinctive or inspired from some ethereal place. But in reality, the teacher is relying on his/her/their vast professional knowledge, not having to think about each of the necessary topics individually because doing so has become habit.

Develop Lengthy Lesson Plans

All student teachers, whether they are preparing edTPA portfolios or not, will be required to create and implement lesson plans as part of their student teaching evaluations and education. In general, the lesson plans you develop for student teaching will be longer and more complex than the plans your cooperating teacher produces each day. Student teaching program/edTPA plans are usually about four pages in length, per day.

The likely discrepancy between the length of your required lesson plans and your cooperating teacher's lesson plans is due to the fact that teachers have to create multiple plans every day, and many use a planning template that does not spell out each intricate detail of the lesson plan.

The reason for this is that they don't need to do that. Over time, teachers rely on their internalized, professional knowledge to guide their planning. In other words, your cooperating teacher holds a lot of what you will be writing down in your plans "in their head," and many master teachers write what look like informal notes for plans. You will surely get to that point in your own teaching with practice and experience.

But for now, the lesson plans you will create for your student teaching course/edTPA portfolio need to clearly articulate several topics that you might not even know you have to plan for. In fact, certain topics, such as academic language, seem almost invisible when you observe a lesson, unless you are looking for it. So at this point in your teaching, you will want to make your thinking about planning visible to yourself and your mentors.

Having a detailed plan with you can also feel reassuring when you are teaching. It serves as a script that helps you remember to ask your deliberately worded questions and provides you with a logical sequence of activities.

How Do You Figure Out What to Teach?

When preparing lesson plans as a student teacher, you will be entering a context in which the curriculum is already established, so it makes sense to use whatever curriculum and materials the class is already using. If, for example, they are working from a textbook or pre-scripted curriculum, you can use that curriculum to provide the structure and content for your lesson plans. If you are teaching in a physical education context, you might not have a written curriculum, but the topics will likely be outlined for the semester. If you are teaching in an ELA context, it is likely that the texts will have been selected, so you will coordinate your lesson plans with the book(s) you are required to teach.

A benefit of using a set curriculum is that it will be easier for you to locate a central topic, follow a logical sequence of learning activities, ensure that your plans are aligned with state/national standards, and that your content is accurate.

The downside is that you don't necessarily get the opportunity to work creatively, devising unique plans that you are excited to try out. Therefore, you will want to ask your cooperating teacher to help you find opportunities to bring your own creative flourishes into your instructional design, as that too is an important teaching skill to develop.

When working with a curriculum that you did not write from scratch, an important challenge is to figure out how to customize aspects of the curriculum by taking your students' prior learning, learning needs, and interests into account. When creating instructional plans, keep in mind what makes the community and school in which you will be teaching distinctive, and make certain that you accommodate the cultural attributes, values, and interests of your students. Also consider how students are grouped and the ways in which curriculum needs to be differentiated (more on that later in this chapter). Questions to help you understand your student teaching context were provided in chapter 1.

You do not need to design your lessons from scratch if you are preparing an edTPA. You can use published lesson plans, as long as you properly cite them.

THE CENTRAL FOCUS

When you create lesson plans within a unit/learning segment, these lesson plans are all organized around a central, organizing learning goal. The edTPA, and therefore many teacher education programs, label this goal the "central focus."[1] As a thesis statement in an essay serves to connect several, related topics, the central focus serves to connect several lesson plans. As you implement your lesson plans, you will prepare your students to demonstrate that they have developed the understandings and skills necessary to meet the goals of your central focus.

When creating a unit/learning segment, it is important to spend some time crafting a central focus that is realistic and elegant, not overly complicated but appropriately challenging. If your central focus is too complex or ambitious, you'll get off track and/or your students won't be able to accomplish that goal. If it's too simple, chances are they will be working primarily with simple skill acquisition and will not be able to engage with more challenging, conceptual work.

Examples of a Strong Central Focus

1. Spanish: Students will be able to write a persuasive letter in Spanish to the school principal about a change they would like to make in the school. Students will use the present perfect tense and vocabulary about school life to *persuade* the principal that their idea is a good one.
2. Physical education: Students will demonstrate how to properly perform exercises for the upper body and lower body using supersets and *explain* how muscles are working in each exercise.
3. Secondary math: Students will apply their knowledge of ratio and proportional relationships to solve a variety of problems involving percentages. They will *describe* how percentages are used in real-world situations.

One way to help you locate your central focus is to imagine the summative assessment that you will administer at the end of your lessons. Are students solving math problems and then explaining their solutions? Are students performing basketball dribbling drills and then describing how to dribble? Are students writing a paragraph about a topic, arranging information on a graphic organizer, or creating a poster or a public service announcement? In addition to whatever prior knowledge your students have, what understandings and skills would your students need to learn in order to meet with success on that assessment?

The Language Function

Now reread the central focus examples above. Notice that each of them has a word such as "explain," "describe," "compare/contrast," "analyze." Those verbs are called *language functions*. The verb describes specifically what students do with language. When you write your central focus, make sure that it includes a language function, because establishing a language function will guide the discipline-specific ways in which your students will work with language throughout your unit/learning segment.

Consider how different it is to *describe* a topic, like how to dribble a basketball, than it is to *retell* a series of events from a particular point of view. Each language function has its own set of language requirements—rhetorical conventions that connect with it.

If one is *describing*, the focus will be on using vivid descriptive language such as adjectives and adverbs. If one is *retelling*, the focus will be on sequencing events, using temporal words (such as "first," "next," "finally"), and selecting which important details to include in the retelling.

In some disciplines, such as physical education or math, students must demonstrate their thinking in the cognitive domain or their conceptual understanding of a topic. So students will likely *describe* a process or *explain* a procedure to make their thinking transparent and connect it to the procedure they are learning to execute.

Once you have composed your central focus and included your language function, you will then assess your students' abilities to work with that particular language function throughout your lesson plans and when you administer the summative assessment at the end of your learning segment. For example, to what extent did your students correctly *retell* the series of events, *explain* the procedure, *describe* the process?

Draft your central focus early on, but know that it may change slightly as you build your lesson plans and assessments around it. Examine your drafted central focus. Does it include a language function? Can you design an assessment at the end of your learning segment that will allow your students to demonstrate that they have achieved this?

Before you move forward to design your lessons, you will need to collaborate with your cooperating teacher or mentor at the school where you are student teaching. Do this early in the process, because your cooperating teacher can project where the class will be in terms of their curriculum around the time when you will be teaching your lesson plans. So for example, if you know that you will be teaching your learning segment in about six weeks, ask your cooperating teacher where the class will be in six weeks and what topic you will be teaching.

If you are preparing an edTPA, let your cooperating teacher know that you need to work with a central focus in mind and that you will need to administer a summative assessment at the end of your learning segment (and collect the assessments for the whole class).

Whether you are preparing an edTPA portfolio or assignments for your student teaching seminar, it is crucial to express to your cooperating teacher that you need to confirm the curriculum topic you will be writing about so that you can spend your time planning without having to make major changes. This information is very useful early on because you want to create appropriate plans, instruction, and assessments for the entire class, but you also need to create appropriate supports for particular groups of students and individuals with particular learning needs. You will have a lot of designing to do.

Below is a checklist that you can use when you speak with your cooperating teacher to make sure you address important planning topics so that you can successfully and efficiently organize your planning.

Important Questions to Ask Your Cooperating Teacher to Help You with Lesson Planning

- Is there any special curriculum that I will need to follow (this would be a program, a textbook, etc.)?
- I want to teach my learning segment (unit) around this particular date (whatever date you and your course instructor have determined). What topic will we be working on then?
- Is there a particular pace at which I have to work? (For example, if your class is on a test-prep schedule and particular topics must be addressed in a particular order and within a particular amount of time, such as one day.)
- Is there an expectation about how students should be grouped? If students are grouped in particular ways, why are they grouped that way? (Oftentimes groupings are based on assessment data, such as assessment results, learning needs, linguistic needs, or common interests.)
- In regard to this group of students and the topic I hope to teach, what relevant prior knowledge do they generally have?
- In regard to this group of students, what confusions or misunderstandings do you think they will have?
- In regard to this group of students, what mistakes might they make?
- What supports can we put in place to help clear up any misunderstandings or mistakes?
- What might my summative assessment be, and when will I administer it?
- What curriculum and materials will I have available to me?
- Is there any information that my cooperating teacher needs that I need to ask my college supervisor/seminar instructor about?

Questions about Differentiation

- Are there any students with special learning needs in this class? Special learning needs include students who are classified with an IEP or 504 plan, or as gifted and talented.
- Other learning needs could be students who are English Language Learners. If you have English Language Learners, you'll want to know their level. Are they newcomers with only a few English words? Are they advanced English Language Learners?
- Are they learners who speak a variant/dialect of English other than what you might read in a textbook?
- You also want to know about learning preferences. Which students prefer visual/auditory/kinesthetic learning experiences? Do you have several students who prefer to approach learning through different mediums/modes? And what about introverted students who need time alone to process information?

Creating the Lesson Plans

Once you have established your central focus and you have an idea about the kind of summative assessment you will administer as evidence of their learning, you can begin to sketch out your lesson plans. Consider how you might break your central focus goal into three to five teaching days. What will students be doing each day in order to move them toward that goal? Are there three to five skills and concepts that you can teach that will accomplish this? Do these skills and concepts build on each other toward what you will ask students to demonstrate on a summative assessment?

Here are some examples of how you might break your central focus goal into several lessons. These examples connect with the central focus examples provided above.

Spanish Central Focus

Students will be able to write a persuasive letter in Spanish to the school principal about a change they would like to make in the school. Students will use the present perfect tense and vocabulary about school life to *persuade* the principal that their idea is a good one.

- Lesson focus for day 1: Students will review the present perfect tense.
- Lesson focus for day 2: Students will be introduced to and will practice new vocabulary words and phrases that relate to school life. They will practice creating sentences about school life in which they use the newly learned words and verbs in the present perfect tense.
- Lesson focus for day 3: Students will be introduced to and will practice vocabulary words and phrases that are used to persuade others.

Once you have an idea of each day's focus, consider the following questions:

- What skills and understandings will your students develop each day?
- How might they practice these?
- How might they demonstrate their learning progress?

Before moving forward, communicate with your cooperating teacher. Ask her or him if your central focus goal and your rough sketch of the lesson plan make sense and will be achievable in terms of who the students in your class are, and also in terms of the school schedule. Make sure you organize this schedule around your student teaching seminar schedule as well. Oftentimes, your seminar instructor or college-based mentor will want to see your lesson plans well before you actually teach them to ensure that your plans are on target.

Materials for Your Lesson Plan

For each lesson plan you create (each day), you should list the materials you plan to use. Materials include books, pages of a particular book, pictures, anchor charts, videos, PowerPoint slides, websites, software, materials for science labs or math explorations, and any other materials that you plan to use during instruction.

How do you select materials to use in your lesson plans? You will use materials that are available to you in your student teaching classroom, obviously, and you will research to find other materials to integrate in your lessons. The materials you select for your lessons *should help your students answer the essential questions* you have identified for each lesson, and they should align with the goal of your central focus. Also, they should appeal to a wide range of students, and you should include variety or choice when possible.

The Lesson-Plan Template

Your student teaching seminar instructor will likely provide you with a detailed lesson-plan template. The following section provides an annotated breakdown of a template that has proven an effective guide for students writing edTPA portfolios, as each topic can be elaborated on in the Task 1, Part E commentary template.

ANNOTATED LESSON-PLAN TEMPLATE

The first part of your plan includes your name, the grade level that you are teaching, and the materials you will use for the particular class. Spend some time thinking about your lesson title. It should capture the main idea of your lesson plan.

Design an Overview of Your Lesson Plan

Before composing a detailed lesson plan, sketch out a general overview of the lesson according to the categories below. This will help you get a sense of the main learning activities and assessments you will use throughout your plan. Pay attention to how long your cooperating teacher spends at the beginning, middle, and end of a typical lesson plan, and try to stick to the same timing.

Table 4.1.

Introduction

How many minutes will it take?	Activities	Assessments used

Middle of Lesson

How many minutes will it take?	Activities	Assessments used

End of Lesson

How many minutes will it take?	Activities	Assessments used

Tips for Your Lesson Overview

- Briefly describe whatever routine you typically follow at the beginning of a class. Your introduction, for example, might include a "Do Now" or anticipatory set.
- Design instructional activities that follow a "gradual release" (I do, we do, you do) progression that focuses on your skills and understandings.
- End with an exit ticket, KWL (know, want to know, learned), or discussion in which you circle back to questions that came up in the introduction where you review the skills and understandings that the class worked with on this day.

Writing Learning Objectives

When writing your learning objectives for the day, identify what you hope students will be able to DO as a result of the instruction—those are the skills and procedures you hope to teach, and what students will be able to UNDERSTAND as a result of the instruction—those are the concepts. However, do not write, "Students will be able to understand." Instead, choose a language function that describes how your students will be able to *express* their understanding. How will you be able to see evidence of their understanding? They might describe, explain, compare, justify, analyze, etc.

Table 4.2.

Learning Objectives	
• Skills/procedures What are the specific skills you will address? • Concepts/understandings What are the specific concepts/understandings you will address? • Essential question What is an essential question that you want to address in this lesson?	
• State Learning Standards and Discipline-Specific Content Standards	
What standard(s) support your learning goals? Include State ESL Standards along with Common Core Standards.	

Tips for Your Lesson Objectives

- Write an objective for an understanding. What will your students understand, and how will they DEMONSTRATE their understanding?
- Make sure your objectives align with your standards and your CENTRAL FOCUS.
- Remember that an objective must be observable and measurable.
- If you are preparing an edTPA, see your handbook to find the specific standards required for your discipline.

Incorporating Academic Language

Table 4.3.

What **language function** do you want students to develop in this lesson?	
What content-specific vocabulary/symbols do students need to know?	
What specific way(s) will students need to use language (**discourse/syntax**)?	
How will you support students so they can understand and use the language associated with the language function and other demands in meeting the learning objectives of the lesson?	

What Is Academic Language?

Academic language is a term that refers to the language that students will learn primarily in educational contexts (school and academic texts). Students will encounter academic language when they read textbooks and observe the teacher or other disciplinary experts work with academic content. Students will develop academic language in the context of working in specific academic disciplines; however, it is not enough to just engage students in the discipline and hope that they acquire academic language in the process. We need to be deliberate and plan ways for students to work with language in both general and discipline-specific ways so that they can successfully understand the topics they encounter in school and successfully express their knowledge about these topics.

Academic language can be general. For example, when writing an academic essay, an author will employ vocabulary words or terms that are more precise and sophisticated than they might employ in a casual conversation with friends. In addition to using a more sophisticated vocabulary, the author will likely use complex sentence constructions that would seem too cumbersome in regular, everyday speech. So part of a teacher's job, regardless of the discipline they teach, is to model general academic language in speech, writing, and in the assigned texts and materials.

Academic language is also discipline-specific. A teacher working in a specific discipline will model a skill or procedure and provide materials to students that highlight discipline-specific academic language features. For example, in ELA, the teacher might show students how to decide whether an example of figurative language is a simile or a metaphor. Those are terms that are discipline-specific and help ELA students analyze literary works.

The edTPA breaks academic language down into helpful subcategories that describe different ways in which students can work with academic language: language function, vocabulary, discourse, and syntax. Each will be described below.

Language Function

As described earlier in this chapter, a *language function* is a verb that describes how students will be working with language. They might *describe, explain, analyze, justify, compare/contrast, identify*, and *interpret* just to name a few. And as described above, the language function should be highlighted in your central focus because it describes how your specific students will be demonstrating their learning.

It is a good idea for the language function you highlight in your lesson plan to be the same one included in your central focus. However, you might want to target a language function that is related to the language function listed in your central focus. For example, if the language function listed in your central focus is "retell," it is possible that on one day, you will be describing a series of events as part of your retelling; on that particular day, you may highlight "describe" as the language function that is taught in service of retelling.

The vocabulary you highlight and the discourse and syntax structures that you engage your students in will help support them to accomplish that language function.

Vocabulary

Vocabulary words and phrases (as well as symbols) are part of the academic language you will target in your lesson plans. Consider ways to teach content vocabulary, such as "vacuum" (science), "quotient" (math), "antagonist" (ELA), and "jump shot" (PE). You will want to provide your students with opportunities to gain exposure to content-specific vocabulary and to both observe and practice using the vocabulary in meaningful, discipline-specific contexts.

In addition to discipline-specific content vocabulary, you may want to highlight vocabulary that students might encounter in the texts and other materials you include in your lesson plan. For example, if a history reading includes vocabulary terms such as "consecutive" or "cursory," you will also want to highlight those words for your students so that they can become familiar with them. There are multiple methods to help students encounter, practice, and learn new vocabulary.

Discourse

In addition to vocabulary terms and phrases, academic language also describes discipline-specific ways of expressing knowledge. Discourse refers to the production of language or output of language in speech or writing, so you will describe the opportunities you have planned for students to engage in discourse. Discourse is discipline-specific in the context of academic language, so consider the ways in which practitioners in your discipline speak or write. For example, historians may engage in the discourse of cause and effect. Therefore, you might establish opportunities for your students to speak or write in ways that help them connect an effect to a particular cause. And you might even set up a structure to support students, such as "One event that occurred prior to the US Civil War was _____, and one effect of this event was _____."

In science, students learn to write lab reports. The common structure of a lab report represents a discipline-specific way of communicating knowledge known as discourse. Discourse is another category we consider when planning academic language. The most important aspect of discourse is that it puts the focus on students producing language to share and articulate their thinking, rather than just listening to a teacher lecture.

Syntax

In addition, students will engage in discipline-specific ways of organizing language to represent their thinking, and this is known as syntax. For example, when a PE student describes how to complete a push-up, they will list each move (cue) in order. If the student makes a mistake when describing that order, the push-up may not be executed successfully. Knowing how to communicate ideas in a particular order, syntax, is an important aspect of academic language.

We use the term "syntax" to describe the order in which we place parts of speech in sentences. For example, in English, we usually place the adjective before the noun, as in "yellow banana." When planning your lessons, think about opportunities you will provide your students to order information. Students engage in syntax when they fill out a Venn diagram or a graphic organizer, when they make a list, when they describe a procedure and order the steps in the procedure, or when they order symbols in an equation.

How Does a Teacher Support Students to Learn Academic Language?

There are numerous ways to support students to use academic language successfully, and you can plan for those in your lessons. The most obvious is that you can plan to circulate and listen to students engaged in turn-and-talk conversations. When listening, you can ensure that students are engaging correctly in the discourse you have assigned, using the vocabulary correctly, and accomplishing the language function you have identified as a goal.

Anchor charts or word walls are examples of materials that you might use to support academic language. Sentence stems, graphic organizers, dictionaries, thesauri, and translations are examples of materials that you might use to support academic language in a lesson. In addition, you might group students intentionally in order to support academic language use. For example, if you are working with emergent bilingual students, you might want to group students who speak the same language together. Or if you are differentiating for specific groups of students, you may have some students working with more difficult vocabulary than other groups.

If you are working with English Language Learners, you will want to identify how you plan to support your ELLs to work successfully with academic language. Perhaps you will be incorporating SIOP (Sheltered Instruction Observation Protocol)[2] for example.

Again, make sure that the vocabulary you plan to teach, as well as learning activities using discourse or syntax, supports students to employ the language function you identified in your central focus.

Table 4.4.

Theory	
Why are the learning tasks for this lesson appropriate for your students? Cite specific theory or a specific theorist to support your assertions.	
Prior Knowledge	
How does this lesson connect with students' prior knowledge?	
Connection to Students	
How does this lesson connect with your students' interests, experiences, and cultural backgrounds?	

Rationale

What Is the Rationale?

When you transition from being a student teacher to a teacher leading your own classroom, you will be asked by school stakeholders, including administrators, parents, students, and other teachers, to provide a rationale for teaching the topics you are teaching, and for using the methods you are using. Certainly you can justify the subject matter and topics you teach by leaning on your state and national standards, but what about your teaching methods? Why, for example, might you have students create a WebQuest rather than take a multiple-choice test?

Regardless of the methods you use, you will need to justify your motivations, so get in the habit of articulating a rationale for your plans while student teaching. This rationale can cover an entire unit or a single lesson, whatever you think is appropriate. When a teacher provides a rationale for their plans, they often cite a particular theory that their work is affiliated with, they cite their students' prior learning, and they cite their students' interests as well. This part of the lesson plan pushes you to describe how these topics justify your plans.

If you are working on an edTPA portfolio, you will be asked to provide a rationale for your planning. This section is designed to help you articulate why you think your plan will serve your students well.

Theory

Once you have an idea of what and how you would like to teach, recall some of the theorists or theories you have met in your methods courses. Can you identify a theory or theorist that you think aligns well with your plan? Can you think of a theorist who would agree with your methods? See the list of theorists and theories in chapter 9 for ideas.

Prior Knowledge

You will likely have taught or observed students working with the topic of the lesson prior to the one you are planning, so state what students have learned *before* this day's lesson—learning that you will be building on in this lesson. How do you know that students have this prior knowledge? You will have observed them demonstrating it, you will have been told by your cooperating teacher, or you will have conducted an assessment (called a pre-assessment) to determine their prior knowledge.

Ensure that you deliberately invite your students to make connections between their prior knowledge so that those connections are clear to them also. You might ask, "Do you remember what we learned about how to multiply fractions yesterday? Well, today, we are going to build on what you learned yesterday."

Connection to Student Interests

It is important to think through and address student interests in your lesson plans so that you get in the habit of deliberately connecting the day's lesson not just to your students' prior learning but to their interests and lives out of school. Again, it is important to make those connections explicit to your students. One way to accomplish this is to design questions that will help you make it very clear that you are deliberately attempting to connect your teaching to your students.

For example, you might ask students a question such as: "How might you apply this idea to your life outside of school?" to establish a connection between your topic and their interests. Perhaps you will reference books that students have read and enjoyed in the past or stories that they know.

Perhaps you will be teaching a sport that is similar to another sport that you know they enjoy. Perhaps you will be making connections between a math topic and items that high school students have to budget for (like cell phone data) or careers that they might be interested in.

Perhaps you are studying a topic that connects to a part of the world that many of your students' families emigrated from. You might even use materials that students are interested in somehow. For example, if you are engaged in a science experiment using a variety of sweeteners, you can ask students which ones they prefer or know about.

Important edTPA Connection

If you are submitting an edTPA portfolio, you must provide evidence in your video recordings that you did indeed make these connections, so designing questions like the ones above to explicitly make the connections will help you when it comes time to prove that you did consider your students' prior learning and interests.

Envision the Lesson Progression

The following section is designed to help you think about how you will progress through your lesson using a gradual release model.

Table 4.5.

How will you start the lesson to engage and motivate students in learning?	Teacher does:	Students do:
What skills/procedures/understandings will you model? How will you model?	Teacher does:	Students do:
What activities will students engage in to meet the learning objectives of this lesson?	Teacher does:	Students do:
What questions will you ask that will invite students to explain what they know?	Teacher does:	Students do:
What questions will you ask that will encourage students to think deeply about the presented materials?	Teacher does:	Students do:
How will you give students the opportunity to practice independently so you can assess and provide feedback?	Teacher does:	Students do:
How will you know when students have achieved the learning objectives of this lesson?	Teacher does:	Students do:
How will you end the lesson?	Teacher does:	Students do:

Starting the Lesson and Engaging Students

The progression begins by encouraging you to articulate how you might begin the lesson in an engaging way that helps motivate students to participate and connect the day's learning to their prior learning and interests.

Modeling

This progression also focuses on modeling. What is a skill/procedure/understanding that you will model during this lesson, and how might you go about doing that? Will you provide a demonstration and take questions at the end? Will you share a text with your students and ask them to help you revise it, modeling how an author uses reader feedback to revise? Will you actually do the modeling, or will you use a video or text?

Engaging Students in the Learning

How will students engage with the lesson? What will they be doing in order to actively participate in the learning? Will they be attempting the same skill/procedure/understanding that you just modeled?

Questions that Inspire Deep Thinking

Questions that encourage students to think deeply are the higher-order-thinking questions described throughout this book. They often begin with "why," or explain and encourage multiple perspectives and conceptual thinking. These questions are connected with those top tiers on the Bloom's[3] taxonomy triangle.

How Do You Know that Students Learned What You Taught?

How will you know when students have achieved the objectives of the lesson? Be very specific about what this will look like in terms of their output. Will they demonstrate learning? Will they solve and explain their solution to a problem? Will they be able to correctly answer questions or perform a task?

Ending Your Lesson

How will you end the lesson in such a way that you circle back to your objectives and debrief with your students about what they learned, what they found interesting/engaging, what still seems challenging for them, and what questions they have for further research? It is important to save three to five minutes per lesson for a brief wrap-up in which you give students some time to reflect. You might have them accomplish this in writing also, using an exit ticket or a KWL, for example.

Consider Differentiation/Planned Supports
Table 4.6.

How will you provide the whole class access to learning based on their needs?	
How will you provide groups of students with similar learning needs access to learning based on their needs?	
How will you provide individuals access to learning based on their needs?	
If you teach ELLs: How will you provide ELLs access to learning based on their needs and varying linguistic levels from beginning to advanced?	

In this section of your lesson, you will consider how you will support your students to successfully meet the lesson objectives. In the academic language section of this plan, you articulated deliberate language supports that you will put in place to facilitate students' academic language learning. In this section, consider more general supports, such as the use of graphic organizers, outlines, modeling, turn-and-talks, checklists, etc. Start by thinking about the supports you are putting in place for your whole class, and then consider groups of students who might need more specific supports or challenges.

If, for example, you have a group of emergent bilingual students who are at the same level, what supports might they need to successfully meet the objectives? If you have a group of gifted and talented students in your classroom, they might need additional challenges in the form of more conceptual work to keep them engaged and on task. If you have students who are struggling readers or who have difficulty with math facts, you will want to put supports in place for them also so that they can be successful.

Perhaps you have an audiobook available for a group of students to listen to or a graphic organizer that you have started for them. Perhaps you have a hundreds board available for students who are still learning their multiplication facts. In a language class, some students might have fewer sentences to write, and in a physical education context, you might have one group that struggles with coordination using beach balls as volleyballs.

Individual supports would be supports or challenges you establish in advance for those individuals who have a particular plan, such as an IEP or 504 plan, or for an individual student who needs his or her work customized to some extent. If, for example, you have a student with attentional challenges, what might you put in place that allows the student to learn through movement?

More on Differentiation and Planning

When you make a plan, address the range of students in terms of their abilities and interests. If you have classified students, students with special linguistic needs, students who are below grade level in reading or math, advanced or gifted students, or students with particular learning preferences that require accommodations or modifications, you will need a specific plan to support and challenge these students. Remember to offer both accommodations (altering the learning environment in some way) and also modifications (altering the learning materials/assessments in some way) as appropriate for the students you are serving. Remember that you must provide accommodations for any students with specific IEPs or 504 plans.

Your cooperating teacher and/or other school personnel discussed in chapter 3 can help you think about how you might make accommodations/modifications for specific students. Below is a sampling of ideas from former student teachers who devised accommodations/modifications and put them in place for their students. The examples are general enough that you can modify for your specific discipline, grade level, and students.

Providing Supports for Students with Special Learning Needs or Learning Preferences

Table 4.7.

Description of Learning Need or Preference	Possible Accommodations/Modifications
For a student with physical limitations	<ul><li>I will modify physical activity with shorter distance, fewer repetitions, modified stretching, and walking instead of running or jumping.</li><li>I will modify equipment, using a larger ball, for example.</li><li>I will focus on one skill/cue at a time.</li><li>I will use diagrams, role-playing, or colors to teach a sequence.</li></ul>
For a student with a visual impairment	<ul><li>I will provide student with preferential seating in terms of proximity to teacher and visuals.</li><li>I will provide large, colorful resources.</li><li>I will provide oral directions.</li></ul>

(continued)

Table 4.7. *(continued)*

Description of Learning Need or Preference	Possible Accommodations/Modifications
For a student who prefers kinesthetic learning	• I will use demonstrations. • I will use role-playing. • I will use manipulatives. • I will allow sketching/doodling while listening. • I will encourage notetaking or having students write out their ideas. • I will allow one particular student to stand up when working independently or walk around in the back of the room as we have planned, as long as this does not bother any other students. • I will provide fidget spinners, beeswax, or squeeze balls to students who need to use them to help them focus.
For a student who prefers auditory learning	• I will read directions. • I will use audio recordings. • I will teach students steps (such as math procedures) that are set to a common melody (*Twinkle Twinkle Little Star* works well) or teach poems that rhyme. • I will invite student to EXPLAIN procedures or orally practice skills/drills (like naming states and capitals).
For a student who prefers visual learning	• I will include anchor charts or PowerPoint slides. • I will include diagrams, maps, or illustrations. • I will invite students to sketch out ideas. • I will color-code text to demonstrate big ideas and connections. • I will use graphic organizers. • I will use anchor charts.
For a student who is an English Language Learner with only a few words of English	• I will preteach and provide vocabulary. • I will group student with other students who speak the same language, so that they can support each other and translate. • I will use partner talk. • I will ask the parents or others who know the student about their interests and integrate them into our learning. • I will give the student some time to practice speaking an answer prior to calling on the student. • I will use visuals, such as pictures. • I will provide translated materials/texts to develop or help student access background knowledge.

Designing High-Quality Lesson Plans

Description of Learning Need or Preference	Possible Accommodations/Modifications
For a student who speaks a variant of English that is not the language used in textbooks	• I will use sentence starters. • I will provide models. • I will use materials, such as an anchor chart, to make vocabulary words and phrases available to students.
For a disconnected/ unmotivated student	• I will encourage them to write or read about an interest they have. • I will use examples to encourage their attention in class. • I will provide student with a "real-life" purpose for engaging with the lesson. • I will highlight the number of correct answers on graded assignments, rather than the number of wrong answers. • I will create interest-specific learning centers in the classroom. • I will provide choice of reading/writing topics when appropriate.
For a student who is advanced and needs extra challenge	• I will challenge this student with learning activities that don't just keep the student busy but require them to solve problems/puzzles. • I will challenge the student to connect the learning to real-world situations or challenges. • I will offer a more complex text. • I will require student to compose a more elaborate/detailed response. • I will challenge the student with work that includes more critical thinking/creativity. • I will *sometimes* pair the student with a student who is struggling so that they can help/teach what they know to another.
For a student who has attentional challenges	• I will provide extra space for the student, and extra space for their materials. • I will move student away from high-traffic areas. • I will stand near the student when giving directions and circle back frequently. • I will provide small, supervised breaks for student. • I will provide extra time at the end of the period for student to organize materials. • I will reduce visual and auditory distractions. • I will invite and support student to "help" me distribute supplies or keep track of time/materials/information.

(continued)

Table 4.7. *(continued)*

Description of Learning Need or Preference	Possible Accommodations/Modifications
For a student who struggles in math	• I will assign fewer problems. • I will space problems far apart or use graph paper. • I will color-code or underline key words in word problems. • I will give the student an opportunity to explain or teach a procedure in order to solidify the process for them. • I will use diagrams, role-playing, or colors to teach a sequence.
For a student who is a struggling writer	• I will provide models so that the student sees how to structure the writing. • I will allow student to dictate ideas or use other alternative genres, such as graphic design. • I will use story or sentence starters. • I will share notes or provide copies of PowerPoints, etc. • I will provide the student an opportunity to "talk through" their ideas before writing them. • I will use graphic organizers to help the student structure their written response. • I will encourage the student to sketch and label or sketch and write.
For a student who is a struggling reader	• I will provide oral information. • I will use audio texts prior to reading. • I will simplify text or directions. • I will preview texts to orient student to layout and big ideas. • I will give student a purpose for reading—something to look for. • I will summarize the text in the context of class discussion. • I will supplement the reading with experiential learning, video or audio recordings, other texts, visuals. • I will include prereading materials such as preteaching vocabulary and content. • I will use role-playing to emphasize important relationships or concepts.
For a student who is introverted	• I will provide student with the option of working alone when possible. • I will provide a location in the classroom where student can have some space. • I will provide time during the class for quiet, individual activity, such as writing (Do Now) time.

Note: These supports will prove effective for individuals with specific learning needs, but many of them are excellent instructional practices that will benefit everyone in your class.

ALIGNMENT

When you create your lesson plans and assessments, take the time to make sure that your central focus aligns with your learning objectives for each day, that your learning objectives align with your disciplinary standards and other requirements, and that the evaluation criteria that you will use to assess student learning align with your learning objectives. Each of these topics work together. This graphic demonstrates how all topics are aligned. The central focus is the big idea upon which the other topics center. They are all aligned with the central focus and also with each other.

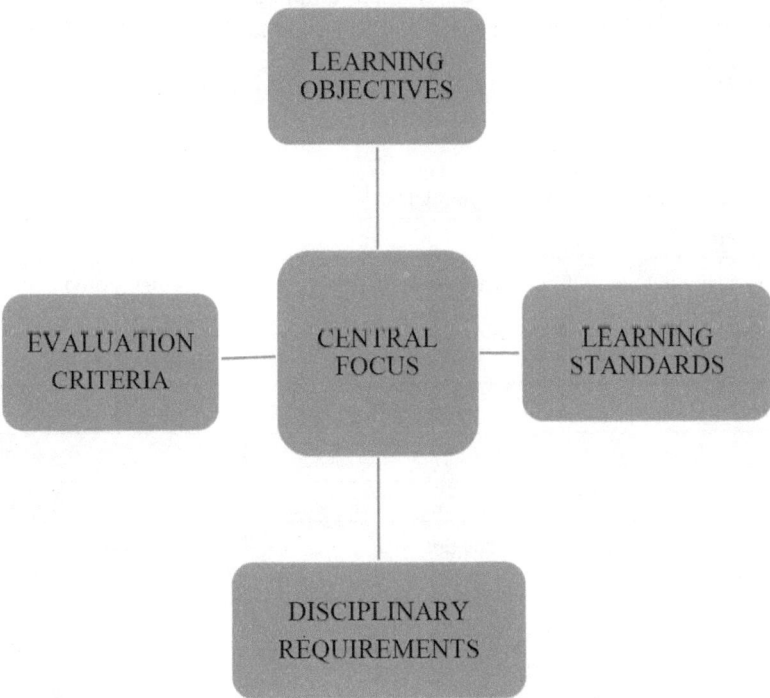

Figure 4.1.

REFLECTING ON YOUR LESSON PLANNING

Once you have mapped out your lesson plans using the lesson-plan template as a guide, review your plans and consider the questions below.

- How does each plan address the central focus, learning objectives, and standards I have selected?
- How are my planned learning activities differentiated to support the learning needs and preferences of my students?
- How do the lesson plans connect with and build on one another?
- Is there a theorist I have studied in my methods courses who would agree with my planning ideas? Why?
- How do my lesson plans support students to learn and use academic language?
- What aspect of my plans will be the most fun or exciting to teach?

See table 4.8 for the entire lesson-plan template.

See the references section for a link to two completed, model lesson-plan templates.

Table 4.8 Detailed Lesson-Plan Template

Introduction

How many minutes will it take?	Activities	Assessments used

Middle of Lesson

How many minutes will it take?	Activities	Assessments used

End of Lesson

How many minutes will it take?	Activities	Assessments used

Objectives

Learning Objectives	
• Skills/procedures What are the specific skills you will address? • Concepts/understandings What are the specific concepts/understandings you will address? • Essential question What is an essential question that you want to address in this lesson?	
State Learning Standards and Discipline-Specific, Content Standards	
What standard(s) support your learning goals? Include State ESL Standards along with Common Core Standards.	

Academic Language

What **language function** do you want students to develop in this lesson?	
What content-specific vocabulary do students need to know?	
What specific way(s) will students need to use language (**discourse/syntax**)?	
How will you support students so they can understand and use the language associated with the language function and other demands in meeting the learning objectives of the lesson?	

(continued)

Table 4.8 *(continued)*

Rationale

Theory and Research	
Why are the learning tasks for this lesson appropriate for your students? Cite specific theory or research to support your assertions. Include theory and research for English Language Learners (ELLs).	
Prior Knowledge	
How does this lesson connect with students' prior knowledge?	
Connection to Students	
How does this lesson connect with your students' interests, experiences, and cultural backgrounds?	

Lesson Progression

How will you start the lesson to engage and motivate students in learning?	Teacher does:	Students do:
What skills/procedures/understandings will you model? How will you model?	Teacher does:	Students do:
What activities will students engage in to meet the learning objectives of this lesson?	Teacher does:	Students do:
What questions will you ask that will invite students to explain what they know?	Teacher does:	Students do:
What questions will you ask that will encourage students to think deeply about the presented materials?	Teacher does:	Students do:
How will you give students the opportunity to practice independently, so you can assess and provide feedback?	Teacher does:	Students do:
How will you know when students have achieved the learning objectives of this lesson?	Teacher does:	Students do:
How will you end the lesson?	Teacher does:	Students do:

Differentiation and Supports

How will you provide the whole class access to learning based on their needs?	

How will you provide groups of students with similar learning needs access to learning based on their needs?	
How will you provide individual access to learning based on their needs?	
How will you specifically scaffold the lesson and include effective practices for ELLS?	

NOTES

1. You can read more about the Central Focus when you register for the edTPA and receive your handbook. Board of Trustees of the Leland Stanford Junior University (2018).

2. Echevarria, J., Vogt, M. E., & Short, D. (2000). *Making Content Comprehensible for English Language Learners: The Siop Model.* Boston: Allyn & Bacon.

3. Bloom, B. S. (1956). *Taxonomy of Educational Objectives, Handbook 1: The Cognitive Domain.* New York: David McKay Co. Inc.

Chapter Five

Designing a Range of High-Quality Assessments

Planning for assessment is a central part of lesson planning. This chapter provides guidance on how to design pre-assessments, formative assessments, and summative assessments for your unit/learning segment and daily lesson plans. This chapter organizes assessment around a three- to five-day unit/learning segment, describing how a teaching candidate can administer one summative assessment at the end of the unit/learning segment and implement several formative assessments throughout each daily lesson plan.

This chapter will support you to accomplish the following assessment goals:

- Aligning your assessments with the unit/learning segment's central focus, learning objectives, and standards;
- Assessing your students' progress with academic language;
- Differentiating your assessments for groups and individual students in your class; and
- Providing frequent, aligned feedback, and including opportunities for students to reflect on their learning and make connections to their interests and prior knowledge.

COLLABORATING WITH YOUR COOPERATING TEACHER

As you start planning assessments, consult your cooperating teacher, who will provide you with important information about your students' prior learning, their interests, and whether or not the assessments you have in mind are too easy or too sophisticated for your students. Your cooperating teacher will provide you with ideas for materials and help you locate those. In addition, your cooperating teacher will likely have ideas about how to modify your assessment ideas to fit the class, groups of students, or individuals in your class.

WORKING WITH A VARIETY OF ASSESSMENTS

The Pre-Assessment

What It Is and What It Does

Many teacher education programs use the term "pre-assessment" to describe an assessment administered to a class *before the actual lesson begins*.

A pre-assessment can be a simple discussion question or a more extensive diagnostic test, but the big idea is to find out what students already know about the topic you will be working with, what understandings they have in relation to your central focus and learning objectives, and what skills they already have in place that you will build on.

In addition, a pre-assessment should also provide you with insight about how the new learning will connect with your students' interests and backgrounds. What do they know and care about, and how might you invite them to bring these interests into your unit or daily plan? Again, this assessment can take many forms, but its purpose is to gain insight about your students' prior knowledge, as well as their interests, so that you can build on what they know and care about.

Formative Assessment

What It Is and What It Does

Sometimes student teachers assume that if they have taught something, their students have learned what was taught. But anyone who has been a student knows that this is not true. Sometimes students learn a part of what has been taught. Sometimes students learn something totally different than what the teacher was trying to teach.

It can be frustrating for both the teacher and the student when a gap exists between what was taught and what was learned. Formative assessments serve to bridge that gap. Formative assessments are not just activities to keep students busy and accountable, they are tools the teacher and students can use to get an accurate understanding of the extent to which students are actually learning what is being taught, the extent to which they are meeting a lesson's objectives. Formative assessments provide evidence of learning—important data for the teacher.

Formative assessments, though they are informal (in other words, not necessarily collected and scored by the teacher), are very important to plan in advance because they provide you with crucial information about student learning throughout your unit/learning segment and daily lesson plan.

Formative assessments make the most sense when you think about them scattered throughout a daily lesson plan, with the purpose of providing you with several check-in points. There is no set number of formative assessments that one should plan for on any given day. However, because formative assessments are often quick and may also include discussion questions, it is reasonable to plan for three to five formative assessments per lesson.

When you consider how many formative assessments can be conducted in a lesson, it is easy to imagine working several assessment opportunities into a day's plan. But what makes these learning activities effective formative assessments? The answer is that each formative assessment is deliberately designed not just to provide students with the opportunity to work with new ideas, procedures, or skills but also to provide the teacher and student with important feedback about how students are progressing in regard to the ideas and skills.

Sometimes students need to have a concept or skill broken down in order for them to understand it. And the teacher won't know how much to break an idea, skill, or procedure down until he or she assesses for understanding. Sometimes students can move through the content at a much faster pace than you anticipated. Even though you will become increasingly better at predicting where students will have confusions, make mistakes, and need strategies and ideas broken down into manageable pieces, you never really know what students need until you assess them. Formative assessments help move us away from assumptions about what our students are learning to evidence of their learning.

Below are some observations that student teachers have made when surveyed about what they learned about using formative assessments in their student teaching classrooms. These observations articulate some important principles of formative assessment.

STUDENT TEACHER OBSERVATIONS ABOUT FORMATIVE ASSESSMENT

- A formative assessment provides important information about where students are and what the next steps should be.
- A formative assessment gives the students a chance to explore ideas and practice skills in a low-stakes and even fun way.

- A formative assessment can be collaborative, which helps students learn how to work together.
- A formative assessment should help both the student and the teacher to better understand how the student is meeting the learning objectives.
- A formative assessment helps the students practice a skill or procedure before the summative assessment.
- A formative assessment shows the learner and the teacher what the students know and are able to do.
- A formative assessment does not include a formal grade.
- Formative assessments happen at various points throughout a unit.
- With a formative assessment, the teacher is looking for something specific (related to the learning objectives of the lesson).
- A formative assessment helps a teacher and student know if the student is not understanding. Then the teacher has the opportunity to reteach or teach the learning objective in a different way.
- Formative assessment is used to monitor student progress throughout the unit, ensuring that the students have the skills and understandings for success on the final task. Formative assessments can empower students because they show students what they learned and what they are still learning.
- Formative assessment gives a better idea of where students are because it doesn't stress them out as much as summative assessments do.

SOME PRINCIPLES FOR DESIGNING AND IMPLEMENTING FORMATIVE ASSESSMENTS

Formative Assessments Align with Learning Objectives

In addition to planning several formative assessments at various "checkpoints" throughout your lesson plan, make sure that you align your formative assessments with the lesson's learning objectives. This takes deliberate planning. If you ensure that your formative assessments provide you feedback about their learning in relation to the learning objectives you have established, then you will not be observing your students complete activities and answer questions in a general way, you will be engaging in targeted observation and listening—observing and listening to see and hear the extent to which your students are understanding the day's learning objectives.

So you won't be circulating through the classroom just randomly checking in with students without purpose. This is why skilled teachers often circulate to observe and listen to students when they are working, with a checklist on a clipboard. They are looking to see if the students are meeting specific criteria.

If, for example, you circulate and note the extent to which each student in your class demonstrates that they understand a particular procedure, you have gained important information. You will know who is ready to move on and who is not, and exactly where those who are not ready are stuck. And you can use your observations to help you determine whether you are ready to move on to the next learning activity and build on what your students have learned, or if you need to reteach. So formative assessments are not random little checks, they are targeted, they are aligned with the day's learning objectives, and they provide crucial checkpoints for both the teacher and student.

Formative Assessments Provide Opportunity for Real-Time Feedback

One benefit of formative assessment is that it provides the teacher with multiple opportunities to provide real-time feedback throughout the class, and if done well, the feedback provides the students an opportunity to pause and assess what they have learned and where they are struggling.

Formative assessments, like all high-quality assessments, provide insights about student learning to both the teacher and students. Formative assessments should be designed to invite conversation between students and between the students and the teacher about the students' learning progress. This communication may lead to the teacher making some revision, either on the spot or the next day of instructional plans, if necessary.

If the teacher uses a higher-order-thinking question and class discussion as a formative assessment of the whole class, the teacher can listen to student responses and communicate with the class about what their responses reveal about what they seem to understand, where are they falling short and why, or where they need additional challenge.

If students compose a formative assessment, such as a graphic organizer, writing a paragraph, or solving a math equation, the teacher can circulate and provide individual *and targeted* feedback as needed.

The teacher should not be the only one providing feedback in the midst of a formative assessment. Students can engage in pair or group conversations, problem solve together, review each other's drafts or work, and the teacher can provide guiding questions to facilitate peer feedback. Getting students in the habit of responding to each other's ideas or work in thoughtful ways can be facilitated by the teacher when the teacher, in conversation with the students, encourages them to go beyond simply saying, "It's good." Feedback conversations can be structured to align with the day's learning objectives.

Digital Technology to Support Formative Assessment Feedback

A teacher can also use digital technologies, such as anonymous polling apps, to survey student understanding and provide feedback. If a quick poll indicates that students are confused about a topic, the teacher can provide the class with additional guidance on the spot. If students are working on Google drive, the teacher can dip in and out of their written responses to provide individual guidance, support, or challenge as needed, so feedback can be immediate.

Formative Assessments Provide Opportunity for Reflection

Formative assessments not only provide the teacher and students with real-time feedback about the extent to which students are meeting the day's learning objectives, formative assessments can also invite students to reflect on their learning. This reflection can occur when students are provided with time to debrief at the end of a lesson, reflecting on how well they met the day's learning objectives and how they might apply what they learned to their authentic, real-world interests.

This can be accomplished in a class conversation, a digital poll, a KWL chart, or an exit ticket, for example. Another way to encourage reflection is to invite students to record "questions for further research" on a poster or sticky notes or in their journal. This helps students reflect on how their learning might connect to other topics of interest.

What Are Some Formative Assessments that Can Be Used in the Classroom?

It is important to know that the actual tool a teacher uses does not determine whether it is or is not a formative assessment. What makes a particular tool (like a graphic organizer) a formative assessment is how it is used. If the assessment meets the criteria described above, it qualifies as a formative assessment.

A teacher could actually use the same tool as both a formative assessment and a summative assessment, but the way in which the tool is used determines the type of assessment it is. If the tool is used to determine how students are progressing in relation to the learning objectives, it is a formative tool. If the tool is used at the end of a lesson or unit to evaluate student progress prior to starting a new topic, it is a summative tool.

Some Formative Assessments

Below is a list of formative assessments that student teachers working in a variety of disciplines and grade levels have used in their instructional plans. Because you will implement several formative assessments over the course of a unit plan, challenge yourself to employ a variety of assessments. Using a variety of assessments will provide access for students with a range of abilities to bring their strengths to the assessment, and the variety will keep them engaged as well.

- Turn and talk
- Think-pair-share
- Graphic organizer
- Solving a series of math problems
- Engaging in an exploration
- Performing a drill
- Responding to a higher-order-thinking question
- Completing an exit ticket
- Group posters or PowerPoints to share learning
- 4-square or other round-robin activities
- Summarize (Tweet)

- 3-2-1 (3 things you didn't know, 2 things you want to learn more about, 1 thing that surprised you)
- Accountable talk
- Thumbs up or thumbs down
- The students will agree or disagree with a response or a statement made by one of their peers
- KWL chart
- Share and Show
- Check for understanding: "What are you doing right now?"

- Teacher questions that are collected and reviewed, completed by a group or individual
- Teacher asks students to guide their work when solving a problem, revising a piece of writing
- Teacher asks students to help identify important criteria needed to successfully complete a particular learning task
- Exit slip
- Reflection
- Journal entry

Digital Ideas

In addition to traditional formative assessments, student teachers have found a variety of digital tools to be useful formative assessments as well. Digital assessments can be helpful because students can use their assessments to pool their ideas and collaborate, provide anonymous responses, and save information to use at a later time. Some examples of digital assessment tools include polling tools such as Nearpod or Kahoot Twitter posts, digital exit tickets with tools such as Spark Post or Socrative, and collaborating tools such as AnswerGarden.

THE SUMMATIVE ASSESSMENT

What It Is and What It Does

Many teachers design units that include a summative assessment, or final demonstration of learning, that will be administered at the end of a unit. The most obvious example is the end-of-unit test. In other words, the teacher considers the final task that his/her/their students will complete to demonstrate the skills and understandings the students have learned over the course of a unit, evaluating student learning of most or all of the unit's learning objectives.

Some teachers use a "backward design"[1] model, starting their planning by first devising a summative assessment; determining what content, understandings, and skills the students will need to successfully accomplish the assessment; and then teaching them everything they will need to know to successfully complete that summative assessment.

Other teachers begin with their learning objectives and build out toward a summative assessment. They consider the skills and understandings they hope to teach, and then devise a summative assessment that will measure the learning. Either way, it is crucial that the summative assessment align with the unit's learning objectives, the central focus, and of course, the disciplinary standards.

There are many options for the format of a summative assessment, such as a graphic organizer, a poster, an essay, or a multiple-choice test. However, a high-quality summative assessment accomplishes two objectives: (1) It does the job of summing up what students have learned in terms of the established learning objectives and usually provides a "final grade," and (2) it provides students with the opportunity to *apply* what they have learned in the unit, sometimes to a new situation or genre.

Applying knowledge and skills to a new situation demonstrates that the students have really internalized the learning. Students might transfer their learning to a new genre, such as a speech or PSA (public service announcement). Oftentimes this transfer involves other disciplines, such as art or ELA, so summative assessments can be interdisciplinary.

Recall the Spanish example in the previous chapter. The student teacher's central focus for her unit was: "Students will be able to write a persuasive letter in Spanish to the school principal about a change they would like to make in the school. Students will use the present perfect tense and vocabulary about school life to *persuade* the principal that their idea is a good one."

The following summative assessment might be used in conjunction with the Spanish central focus and learning objectives:

The summative assessment will be a draft of a persuasive letter in which the students use the present perfect tense, vocabulary and phrases related to school life, and persuasive language to persuade our school principal to make a change to school life.

Notice that the learning objectives are written into the description of the summative assessment, and the students are applying their learning to a new genre—the interdisciplinary task of writing a letter, interdisciplinary because students are engaged in a genre study, which is usually affiliated with ELA. This summative assessment is particularly strong also, because the students are applying their learning about Spanish grammar to an authentic topic that they care about and are provided some choice about the content of their letter.

Ideas for Summative Assessments

- A multiple-choice test
- An essay
- A newspaper article
- A letter to the editor
- A poster
- A public service announcement
- A speech
- A graphic organizer, such as a Venn diagram
- A poem or short story
- A skit or play
- A digital story
- A math test that includes procedural problems, problem solving (like word problems), and a requirement that students EXPLAIN, using math vocabulary, the procedure or their solution to a problem
- A lab report
- A model
- A website

Digital Ideas

Many teachers use digital technology to support summative assessments, such as WebQuests, digital posters on Glogster, PowerPoint, Prezi, screencasts, or digital stories/short films.

It is important to remember that even if you choose a "creative" summative assessment, you must score this using your established learning objectives. You should use a checklist or a rubric that includes evaluation criteria that align with the objectives you have established for your unit.

Summative Assessment Feedback

Feedback will be explored in depth in chapter 6, but you will want to have a clear plan for providing students feedback when you plan out your assessment design.

Ronald's Story

Ronald, a student teacher in a high school English class, administered a summative assessment toward the end of his semester-long placement. He assigned an essay on the novel *Animal Farm*. When Ronald collected the essays and took them home to score, each one took almost forty-five minutes, and Ronald found himself spending a great deal of time correcting mechanics and providing individual comments throughout each student's paper. Then Ronald attached a letter grade to each essay, based on his impression of the assessment's quality.

When Ronald returned the essays to the students, they were upset with him because they could not understand why some students earned different letter grades. When the students challenged Ronald about this, he did not have a clear answer and he felt uncomfortable and defensive.

The next time Ronald assigned an essay, he created a rubric for the essay and shared that rubric with the students when he assigned the essay. The rubric highlighted the learning objectives that Ronald and his class had been working on. When it was time to collect and grade the essays, Ronald found that his response time was significantly shorter because the rubric provided him the guidance for his comments in terms of both the content and the language. When he returned the essays, students had a clear understanding of what they had done well and where they struggled, because they were familiar with the evaluation criteria and Ronald's feedback was consistent when they compared (which students often do) their feedback.

Ronald's story serves as a reminder too that it is only fair to let students know in advance how you will be scoring their assessments, and what kind of feedback they can expect. For example, if you plan to use a rubric or checklist as a tool to score your summative assessment, make sure you provide that tool to your students in advance so that they can see how they will be scored and review each of the evaluation criteria (also your learning objectives) prior to completing the assessment. That ensures transparency and also helps to reinforce the objectives of the learning.

In addition to using a rubric or checklist tool, plan to include a "glow" and a "grow" comment that is written in response to the individual student. These comments should be specific and aligned with the learning objectives rather than cursory ("Good job!"). It is a good idea to provide each student with the completed rubric or checklist and two sticky notes, a "glow" and a "grow" that they can then place in a journal or notebook or in their desk. Whatever your feedback plan, ensure that your feedback is aligned with your learning objectives and not just random, vague feedback.

Planning for Reflection

In addition to figuring out in advance how you will provide meaningful feedback to your students, also plan how you will structure a time and way for students to reflect on what they learned in your unit/learning segment, how they applied their learning to the summative assessment, and how they will make use of the feedback you provided them going forward. Perhaps you will invite each student to engage in an individual conference with you, perhaps they will record goals that are associated with the central focus/learning objectives going forward, or perhaps they will describe their learning in a journal entry.

However you structure their reflection, it is crucial that students have the opportunity to reflect on their progress so that they understand what they learned, can set goals to apply feedback, and make connections to their prior learning and interests.

PLAN TO ASSESS ACADEMIC LANGUAGE

When planning your assessments, no matter the type, make sure that you structure opportunities to assess your students on your stated learning objectives related to the academic language you have targeted in your lesson plans. Remember that you might introduce a new vocabulary term in the context of a discussion about your content, and that term definitely qualifies as academic language. However, the academic language you will want to assess is the academic language that connects with your central focus and your learning objectives.

Your students' ability to use academic language to convey their developing understandings provides you with important insight into how well they are understanding the material. That is why you should monitor how your students use the academic language you have targeted in your unit/lesson plans.

If you have aligned your academic language goals for your students with your learning objectives, it will seem as if the integration of academic language and the learning objectives are identical. For example, if an ELA teacher has established the goal of having students *retell* a story in which students accurately sequence events, use temporal words in their retelling, and retell a story using descriptive language, one can clearly see that the ELA learning objectives involved in the retelling are also academic language goals.

The teacher will assess the extent to which students can *retell* a story (language function), correctly sequence events in a list or on a graphic organizer (syntax), retell an event using descriptive details (discourse), and employ temporal words accurately (vocabulary).

Assessing Prior Knowledge of Academic Language

Have a plan to assess your students' prior knowledge of all categories of academic language that you want to highlight in your unit/lesson plan. You might assess this all at once at the beginning of a unit, or you might target a different skill (such as using temporal words when retelling a story) and its associated academic language category on a different day of your unit.

Once you determine the extent to which your students can successfully work with the academic language you have targeted, you will be able to determine in what ways you can challenge them and build on what they already know. For example, if your students demonstrate that they can easily retell a story and accurately employ the temporal words "first" and "next," you might want to challenge them to learn more sophisticated temporal terms, such as "initially," "finally," or "suddenly."

A pre-assessment will also help you predict where errors or confusions might occur so you can plan to address those. For example, if you administer a pre-assessment and determine that students can accurately retell the events in a story but forget important details, you might design an activity or tool (such as a graphic organizer) to help them record these details so that they can use those supports when retelling.

Formative Assessments Provide Information about Academic Language Learning

In addition to examining your students' prior knowledge of academic language, use formative assessments to help inform you about how students are progressing in terms of their abilities to work with the academic language you have highlighted in your lesson plans. You can use formative assessments to determine the extent to which your students are learning to recognize and accurately use the vocabulary you have taught them.

For example, you might give your students an informal vocabulary quiz or an assignment in which they write original sentences using the newly introduced vocabulary terms. You might even ask them to write a summary of their learning on an exit ticket, using the vocabulary you worked with in the lesson. You can also have students engage in a turn-and-talk discussion and ask them to use newly learned terms in their conversations.

You can listen to these conversations while you circulate to determine if students are using the terms accurately. Another creative formative assessment is to have students draw an illustration of a term's meaning in their journals to illustrate their understanding of new vocabulary, or to have them play a quick game of charades in which students act out a vocabulary word, phrase, or symbol.

You can also use formative assessments to help inform you about how students are progressing in terms of the discourse structures you are employing in your lesson. You can use whole-class discussions to help students practice discourse while simultaneously assessing them. For example, if you want your students to retell a story using descriptive detail, you might have a few students try that during a class discussion.

You can use a turn-and-talk or group conversation to practice discourse. You might also have students write a paragraph in which they demonstrate their ability to employ the type of discourse you have targeted. You might ask students to write a paragraph retelling an event, analyzing a cartoon, explaining how to execute a procedure, or justifying an opinion.

When you review the assessment, you will be looking to see if students are working successfully with whatever content you are teaching, but also you will look to determine how well they can employ the discourse you have modeled for them and are teaching them.

Use formative assessments to help you understand the extent to which students are ordering language (and therefore thinking, since language represents thinking) using the syntax structures you have provided them with. Again, when you assess your students, your focus will likely be on both the content you are teaching and on how successfully students can make a list, accurately fill out a Venn diagram, place symbols in the correct order when writing an equation, and/or fill out a graphic organizer in which they identify a text's main ideas and supporting details.

Assess Academic Language in Summative Assessments

When you design a summative assessment for a unit/learning segment, you will assess the skills and understandings articulated in your central focus and learning objectives. You will also examine how well your students work with the language function you highlighted. You will want to analyze your students' abilities to accomplish that language function. For example, to what extent can they "retell" a story? In a summative assessment, your language function should mirror the language function you included in your central focus, and students should demonstrate that they can work with the associated vocabulary, discourse, and the syntax that you have identified as associated with the content you worked with in your plan. All of those categories support your students' abilities to work with the language function.[2]

DIFFERENTIATION

Just as you try to differentiate your lesson plans to support and challenge all of your learners, you will likely need to differentiate your formative and summative assessments as well. Remember that with assessment, you want all of your students to demonstrate their learning in terms of the learning objectives you have established—everyone needs to work toward those learning objectives and everyone needs to have the opportunity to achieve those objectives. But, of course, not everyone needs to get to them in exactly the same way.

You want your students to be successful, so you will need to set them up for success and modify or adapt the assessments as needed. Advanced learners, such as those who are gifted and talented, reading above grade level, solving math problems quickly and accurately, or who are advanced athletes or artists should be required to meet the learning objectives you have established, but they should be appropriately challenged along the way. This means that you will want to modify their assessments somewhat. How might you do that?

Caroline's Story

Caroline, who was student teaching in a middle school social studies class in which three students were "gifted and talented," had not addressed "gifted education" in her teacher preparation program. As she got to know the students, she noticed that the three easily completed the class work she assigned and then, bored and distracted, they disrupted the learning of others in the class. Caroline consulted with her cooperating teacher, who recommended that Caroline try the following methods:

Compact the learning for those students by presenting them with the most difficult work first and eliminating activities that they can already do. For example, rather than have her students locate countries on a map, Caroline asked them to locate the coordinates for each country's capital cities.

Caroline's cooperating teacher also advised her to provide the three students with less skill work, if they could demonstrate that they already had the target skills, and more sophisticated, conceptual work. So rather than have the three students read and answer questions about key figures of the American Revolution, Caroline asked each student to research a key figure and write a résumé for them, presenting themselves as applicants for the job of most iconic figure of the American Revolution. She had each student make their case and the other students in the class vote on the most iconic.

Caroline's cooperating teacher also asserted that "gifted" students appreciate not just opportunities to engage in creative work but also to engage emotionally and imaginatively with topics of study. So Caroline asked her whole class to write skits or poetry or to produce visual art representing key moments from the history topics they studied.

When planning for her "gifted and talented" students, Caroline also provided them opportunities to work together in class so that they could challenge one another. Caroline determined that the alternative plans she offered those three students were also appealing to many other students in her class so, over time, she offered the kinds of extensions described above to all students, as appropriate.

English Language Learners need language support in order to complete the assessments and demonstrate what they know. How might you accomplish that?

Russelly's Story

When Russelly started her fall student teaching placement on the first day of school, her cooperating teacher told her that the school was overwhelmed with new students for whom English was not their first language, and that they all felt unprepared to serve the students. Though this was challenging for school personnel, Russelly was able to collaborate with other teachers to figure out some effective practices for supporting ENL (English as a New Language) student learning.

They experimented with several methods but ultimately decided that, for Russelly's class, they would use the following supports: Place a strong emphasis on building background knowledge, provide word banks for students so that they could practice using the academic vocabulary, simplify the language in presented readings and other class materials, assess ENL students primarily on their ability to demonstrate that they understood the main concept or idea by focusing on content rather than mechanics, assess assignments composed in the students' native language when possible, reduce the number of problems or sentences required on an assessment, employ more visual assessments such as posters or drawings, and highlight the main words in directions provided on assessments.

Other Considerations

What about struggling readers, struggling math students, students with dysgraphia, students who lack coordination, and students with specific IEPs or 504 plans? How might you provide them with the supports they need in order to most effectively demonstrate the progress they have made and what they have learned?

The answer to this question will be highly individualized because classified students' accommodations will be documented, and they must be followed. However, you can add other accommodations if you feel they are helpful. For example, providing students who struggle to produce writing with an opportunity to share what they know orally may not be an accommodation recorded on an IEP or a 504 plan, but if you believe it is a support that helps a student, employ it.

Another way to differentiate your assessments is to offer choice to students when appropriate. If you can assess the same learning objectives in different forms, it makes sense to give students some choice about how to demonstrate their learning. For example, one student might prefer to share their learning by writing and performing a skit, another student would prefer to write an essay, and another might want to create a poster or graphic to demonstrate the same skills and understandings.

It makes sense to offer choice, because choice helps motivate students, enables them to play to their strengths and interests, encourages divergent (creative) thinking, and can develop their confidence in regard to the learning objectives.

MAPPING OUT YOUR OVERALL ASSESSMENT DESIGN

One key student teaching task is to plan out the assessments you will use each day, throughout your unit/learning segment. When you design a unit or learning segment, you will plan out learning objectives, instructional activities, and assessments. A table can be used to help you map out your assessment plan for each lesson you teach.

Below are examples from the assessment plans of four different student teachers using the same table to organize their assessment plans. Notice that this table guides you to articulate the specific learning objectives each assessment measures, how you will differentiate the assessment for particular students or groups of students, and what academic language you want to assess as well.

Here is an example of a student teacher's assessment map for the second lesson in an ELA unit on character development. Her students had learned how to identify and describe the external traits of people and characters on the previous day. For this lesson, her learning objective was for students to be able to identify and describe the internal traits of people and characters.

This example comes from a student teacher working in a high school living environment classroom. This is the second lesson plan in a unit/learning segment on biome. The student teacher was working toward the following learning objectives:

- Students will be able to describe the features of biome.
- Students will be able to read about a biome and write research questions about one biome.
- Students will be able to create a plan to find out the answer to their research questions.

This example was created by a student teacher working in a middle school PE class. This lesson plan was part of a larger unit on football. The student teacher was working toward the following learning objectives:

- Students will be able to properly and consistently throw an overhand spiral pass.
- Students will be able explain how to properly throw an overhand spiral pass.

This final example comes from a ninth grade math class in which the student teacher was working toward the following objectives:

- Students will be able to identify the domain and range of a quadratic function.
- Students will be able to evaluate a quadratic function for any value of x using substitution method.
- Students will be able to analyze data and mathematical representations.
- Students will be able to explain how they identify the domain and range for quadratic functions, evaluate a quadratic function for any value of x using substitution method, and analyze data and mathematical representations.

Though it seems like quite an effort to create a plan such as this, the effort will pay off because you are working strategically, and, therefore, your assessment plan will be strong and will serve your students well. Your assessments are aligned, they are varied, they are differentiated if need be, and you are assessing for academic language. And again, working in this way will soon become habit, and you, like your cooperating teacher, will have these important considerations "in your head" as you continue to practice them.

Table 5.1.

Assessment Title: Pre-assessment or summative?	Brief Description	Adaptations/ Modifications and for Whom	Provides Evidence of What Learning Objective?	Academic Language Assessed
• Discussion question (Pre-assessment)	• Yesterday we discussed how people and characters have external traits. Can you provide an example of an external trait? • Today we will discuss internal traits. What are some internal traits that characterize people or characters? • Students will turn-and-talk and then share ideas, which will be recorded on the SMART Board.	• For this turn-and-talk, I will have students discuss the question with their pre-assigned discussion partners.	• This will inform me about how much students remember about yesterday's learning objective, and what they already know about internal character traits.	• Discourse (turn-and-talk) • Vocabulary (character, internal trait, external trait)
• Graphic Organizer on a Character's Internal Traits (Formative)	• Students will identify the internal traits their character possesses and list them on the graphic organizer.	• I will provide my English Language Learners an anchor chart with adjectives that they can select to describe their character.	• This assessment will help me determine if students can identify and describe internal character traits. • This assessment will help me determine if students can locate	• Language Function (Describe a character.) • Vocabulary (Use adjectives to describe the character.) • Vocabulary (Use the terms "internal" and "external traits" correctly.)

Designing a Range of High-Quality Assessments 99

		• I will provide sentence starters for my struggling writers. • My advanced students will be grouped together and challenged to identify and describe both the internal and external traits of a character.	textual evidence to support their descriptions of internal character traits.	• Discourse (This assessment will help me determine if students can describe a character they have read about.) • Syntax (Correctly list the internal traits on a graphic organizer.)
		• I will challenge my advanced readers to not only describe the internal traits of a person they know well, I will ask them if they consider these traits to be positive or negative. • For my ENL student, I will provide her with fill-in-the-blank sentences and a short list of adjectives to choose from.	• This will help me determine how much each individual can apply their understanding of internal traits to their own lives.	• Discourse (This assessment will help me determine if students can describe a character they have read about.) • Vocabulary (Use the terms "internal" and "external traits" correctly, as well as adjectives.)
Exit Ticket: • Describe three internal character traits that someone you know well has, and how you know they have these internal traits (formative).	• Students will describe three internal traits in a short paragraph.			

Table 5.2.

Assessment Title: Pre-assessment or summative?	Brief Description	Adaptations/ Modifications and for Whom	Provides Evidence of What Learning Objective?	Academic Language Assessed
• Do Now: "What are some categories we use to describe biomes? What are some factors that would make one biome different from another? What biome are you most interested in?" (pre-assessment)	• These questions invite students to review learning from the previous day, when we learned about the different biomes. Students will write their response in their journals. They will work in groups based on the biome that interests them the most.	• Provide a vocabulary list for ENL students. • Provide an anchor chart for all students, so that they can recall the biomes. The anchor chart has some translated words to support ENL students. • Student with dysgraphia will record her ideas on her laptop, where she keeps her science journal.	• The extent to which students can recall their prior learning about biomes and identify an interest about biomes.	• Language function (describe). • Vocabulary (terms related to biomes: forest, aquatic, grassland, tundra, marine, flora, fauna, geology, soil, temperature, climate, relief). • Discourse (Students answer the questions in writing.)
• After reading about their biome, students will work in groups to discuss, and each student will write a series of questions about their assigned biome in groups (formative).	• Questions will be collected at the end of class to check for progress of individual students.	• Provide students who completed the task with "Depth of Knowledge" graphic organizer to encourage higher-order thinking. • Request tenth graders to help ninth.	• Students will write questions about an assigned biome using the Question Formulating Technique and visual aids. • Students will revise their formulated	• Vocabulary (terms related to biomes: forest, aquatic, grassland, tundra, marine, flora, fauna, geology, soil, temperature, climate, relief).

Designing a Range of High-Quality Assessments

	Allow students to write in native language. Provide space especially for translating categories/topics of research on the table on QFT worksheet. • Provide a vocabulary sheet with definitions of important key words. • I will circulate and guide students not to write too many close-ended questions that can be answered with a "yes" or "no." • I will circulate and make sure questions are researchable.	questions by making them specific.	• Discourse (Students create questions in both speech and writing.)
	• Students can use the supports offered during the class to compose the Exit Ticket. • I will circulate and make sure questions are researchable. • Student with dysgraphia will write her Exit Ticket on her laptop and e-mail it.	• Students will strategize about how to use their formulated questions about their assigned biomes.	• Vocabulary (terms related to biomes: forest, aquatic, grassland, tundra, marine, flora, fauna, geology, soil, temperature, climate, relief.) • Discourse (Students answer the questions in writing.)
Exit Ticket: • What two questions interest you the most, and how might you go about answering them? (formative)	• Students will complete and submit the Exit Ticket.		

Table 5.3.

Assessment Title: Pre-assessment or summative?	Brief Description	Adaptations/ Modifications and for Whom	Provides Evidence of What Learning Objective?	Academic Language Assessed
• Lesson 1 Q&A (pre-assessment)	• Teacher will ask students if they know what an overhand spiral pass is, and why it's an effective pass, or if they have ever seen one thrown on TV or elsewhere.	• Teacher will demonstrate the pass for visual learners. • Teacher will use wait-time to give everyone a chance to think of a response.	• Provides the teacher with an understanding of what students already know and their interest/ knowledge of football.	• Vocabulary (overhand spiral pass).
• Lesson 1 Checklist (formative)	• Assess students' performance ability on properly throwing a spiral football pass. The teacher will be looking for proper use and description of cues when students demonstrate and explain how they executed the pass.	• Different sized (smaller) balls for students who need them. • Short distance throwing for students who need a shorter distance. • Longer distance throwing for advanced students.	• Students will properly demonstrate how to throw a football overhand spiral. • Students will be able to properly demonstrate the overhand football spiral throw 7–10 times. • Students will explain the cues/ mechanics necessary to throw an overhand spiral.	• Vocabulary (the cues for the overhand, spiral pass). • Language function (explain). • Discourse (explaining how to throw an overhand spiral pass).

| Lesson 1 Exit Ticket (formative) | • Exit slip that measures students' ability to explain the proper cues for throwing an overhand, spiral pass.
• Students will have to write down the five cues on throwing a football.
• Students will also be asked what they found difficult and easy about this pass. | • Translated material for ENL students.
• Extra time for struggling writers.
• Visual cues to support students who have a hard time remembering newly learned material. | • Students will explain the cues/ mechanics necessary to throw an overhand spiral. | • Vocabulary (the cues for the overhand, spiral pass).
• Discourse (explaining how to throw an overhand spiral pass).
• Language function (explain). |

Table 5.4.

Assessment Title: Pre-assessment or summative?	Brief Description	Adaptations/ Modifications and for Whom	Provides Evidence of What Learning Objective?	Academic Language Assessed
• Q&A (pre-assessment)	• Teacher will pose a problem and ask the students the following: How do we look for domain and range in a linear function? What axis do we need to look at in order to find the domain and range?	• Students will be required to first discuss the question in their groups, so that students who need time to process before sharing in the large group have some time. • Vocabulary terms will be posted so that students can reference them during the discussion.	• Students will be able to identify the domain and range of a quadratic function.	• Language function (explain). • Vocabulary (domain, range, linear, quadratic, axis). • Discourse (Students will explain the procedure).
Questioning and Feedback (formative)	• Teacher will circulate and ask each group to explain the procedure they are using to solve the assigned problems. Teacher will provide immediate feedback and assistance.	• I will focus on the Station 1 group, because this is the group that struggles the most.	• Students will be able to identify the domain and range of a quadratic function. • Students will be able to evaluate a quadratic function for any value of x using substitution method. • Students will be able to analyze data and mathematical representations.	• Language function (analyze and explain). • Vocabulary (domain, range, linear, quadratic, axis). • Discourse (Students will explain the procedure).

Designing a Range of High-Quality Assessments   105

			- Language function (explain). - Vocabulary (domain, range, linear, quadratic, axis). - Discourse (Students will explain the procedure).
		- Students will be able to explain how they identify the domain and range for quadratic functions, evaluate a quadratic function for any value of x using substitution method, and analyze data and mathematical representations.	
	- Students can write whatever they want to, so if students have any questions about the day's lesson, they can ask it here and I will answer it the following day. - Students can write in their home language if they wish. - Students can use the posted vocabulary as well as their notes and the work they completed in their groups for support if the need it. - Advanced students will be asked to compare the domain and range of quadratic functions and linear functions.		
Journal Entry (formative)	- Teacher will assign a brief (5-minute) journal entry that allows students to summarize what they learned. - Students would be required to explain how they find domain and range for quadratic functions.		

EDTPA CONNECTION

If you are preparing an edTPA, the table above will have a very practical application. The edTPA requires candidates to upload an assessment plan separately from the lesson plans, even though both topics are integrated during instruction. If you are preparing an edTPA portfolio, your assessment plan for the learning segment will be submitted as Task 1, Part 3. You will submit your assessment plan as a Word document with your portfolio.

Candidates find that if they include a complete table for all of their planned assessments, like the one above, and then include blank examples of the assessments they plan to use, they clearly represent their assessment plan.

So when you put your assessment plan together for Task 1, Part 3, you should include all assessments, including formative assessments, such as questions you plan to ask and possible answers, as well as turn-and-talks and possible responses in your assessment plan. Also, you should include your summative assessment (and any differentiated versions of it) that you plan to administer at the end of the unit as well.

Remember that you don't have to create your assessments from scratch, especially if you have quality assessments that have already been developed by your cooperating teacher or a publishing company.

REFLECTING ON THE CHAPTER

Have you ever had a teacher who assumed that just because they taught something you actually learned it? What is the connection between assessment and learning? How will you intentionally design a variety of assessments so that you can consistently monitor student learning and gain direct evidence of learning?

NOTES

1. Grant Wiggins and Jay McTighe, *Understanding by Design* (Alexandria, VA: ACSD, 2005).

2. The academic language topics described in this chapter are informed by the edTPA handbooks and the learning commentary (Task 1) and assessment commentary (Task 3) templates.

Chapter Six

Designing High-Quality Instruction

Once you have designed a strong, detailed plan, it is time to implement it. One college supervisor asserts, "Effective student teachers do more than create wonderful lesson plans, they know how to implement them in a logical way." Designing thoughtful lesson plans is crucial, but how does one successfully implement these instructional plans? And what does effective instruction actually look like?

In this chapter, effective instruction is broken down into several categories to be analyzed. These categories are inspired by common evaluation criteria used in teacher education programs and also the Task 2 (Instruction) prompts in the edTPA. The criteria are listed below, and each will be elaborated on in this chapter.

1. The student teacher demonstrates that they can create and maintain a positive classroom environment.
2. The student teacher demonstrates that they can provide students with appropriate, learning-objective aligned challenges.
3. The student teacher demonstrates that they can engage students in learning objective aligned activities.
4. The student teacher demonstrates that they take students' interests and experiences into account when providing instruction.
5. The student teacher demonstrates that they can effectively model a skill or strategy.
6. The student teacher demonstrates that they can successfully differentiate in order to manage the learning of all students by supporting and challenging students who need specific supports/challenges.
7. The student teacher demonstrates that they can offer students some choice regarding their approach to the activities.

8. The student teacher demonstrates that they can guide students to deepen their learning by structuring conversations around higher-order-thinking questions.

Since this chapter is all about implementing your instructional plans, use the presented ideas to help you target specific instructional practices and "show off" your strengths so that you will have a strong video recording, an outstanding live evaluation, or even an outstanding demonstration lesson for a future job interview.

Much of this advice parallels what student teachers preparing the edTPA will need to demonstrate in their video clips, so that is even more incentive for you to intentionally plan for exemplary moments like the ones described in this chapter.

Regardless of how you must demonstrate the successful implementation of your lesson plans, the descriptions and analyses below will guide you to successfully implement your instructional plans.

CREATING AND MAINTAINING A POSITIVE CLASSROOM ENVIRONMENT

A cooperating teacher asserts, "Effective student teachers smile and appear happy when they interact with students. They enjoy working with students and have positive relationships." This idea underscores the importance of effectively managing the learning environment because, no matter how extraordinary a lesson plan is, if the environment is not conducive to effective instruction, the lesson plan will go nowhere.

CLASSROOM MANAGEMENT

A college supervisor states, "Effective student teachers are not meek. They are friendly with the students, but they employ classroom management strategies with confidence." When you begin student teaching, classroom management will likely be your primary concern. If your cooperating teacher has classroom management procedures in place and they seem effective and ethical (meaning that no one gets hurt or humiliated), you should use those procedures, therefore maintaining consistency in the classroom. Some popular classroom procedures used by both elementary and secondary teachers include the following:

- Clapping a rhythm that your students need to complete in order to get their attention.

- Using a rhyme: "one-two-three all eyes on me."
- Counting down from five.
- Teaching students sign language so that they indicate their need to you rather than verbally disrupting the class.
- Providing "very important information" in a very low whisper in order to get the attention of your students.
- Some teachers use point systems, such as "sweet points," awarded for positive actions and behaviors—positive reinforcement.
- Some teachers employ digital apps, such as Dojo, to assign positive reinforcement and communicate with parents in real time.

In addition to some of these attention-getting procedures, successful management incorporates clear and consistent routines for ordering classroom life. Having a procedure to deal with tardy students so that they don't disrupt the class, requiring the storing of cell phones so that students don't get distracted by them, asking questions, distributing materials, and managing transitions can all have procedures connected with them so that students always know what they need to do and don't find themselves unsure of what to do and frustrated.

It is important to remember that even if you don't feel confident engaging in classroom management procedures, "fake it 'til you make it." You will soon find that students will respond, and your confidence will grow.

Avoid Teaching with a Bee in the Room

One college supervisor observes, "Effective student teachers NEVER speak when the students are talking over them." Another version of this is, "Effective teachers never teach when there is a bee in the room." You won't be able to get or maintain student attention if there is a bee darting around the classroom or anything else that is distracting students to such an extent that they cannot focus their attention on learning.

Effective teachers solve the problem of "the bee" before they give instructions or continue with a lesson. If "the bee" is that students cannot settle down, the teacher waits until he or she has everyone's attention. Do not be afraid to remain silent and wait until you have the focus of your class. It is fine and very effective to stop and wait for attention. When you do so, maintain a neutral (not angry) expression, wait until you have attention, and then just pick up without comment on the disruption.

As a student teacher, try not to start giving directions when students are still talking. Wait until you have their attention, period. If you don't, students will quickly get in the habit of talking over you. This connects to the following advice from a college supervisor: "Effective student teachers give clear directions and make sure everyone understands them before they get started."

Don't Take the Rope

One cooperating teacher advises her student teachers to remember the following advice: "Effective student teachers never take the rope." This statement really gets to the heart of many struggles that new teachers have with classroom management. Taking the rope is a metaphor for attempting to engage in a power struggle with a student.

Imagine a tug-of-war. If a student challenges your authority, don't pick up that rope and engage in that tug-of-war because, even though you have more power as a student teacher (you can get the student in trouble), if you allow yourself to enter a power struggle, you may get upset, lose your temper, and then humiliate or really anger a student. You will likely drop your professional demeanor, thereby sacrificing a bit of your dignity and your students' trust that you are a reasonable, calm person who cares about them. They may not feel safe with you as a result.

RESPECT

The majority of student teachers are excited and happy to work with students. Their exuberance makes the class fun, and students often enjoy working with student teachers as a result. Some student teachers, however, especially if they are working in classrooms where the cooperating teacher is particularly strict, emulate the teacher's style. And though it is natural to want to please the cooperating teacher, if you find yourself with someone who is authoritarian, who humiliates students, and who "rules by fear," don't act that way also, especially if it is not in your nature to do so.

Smile at your students, greet them, thank them for sharing, highlight the positive things they say and do, and treat them with respect. Encourage them to treat each other with respect as well. This takes confidence, practice, and leadership, but your instruction will be more effective if you work to create strong, positive relationships with your students. They will be willing to engage, share their ideas, and take risks.

What Respect Looks Like

Cooperating teachers and college supervisors assert that one can recognize a classroom in which the student teacher maintains respect with and among students because they observe the following:

- The student teacher addresses students by name.
- The student teacher thanks students for participating.
- Students raise their hands and wait to be called on before speaking/responding.
- Students may not raise their hands, but they engage in a conversation in which they do not interrupt each other.
- The student teacher praises students' efforts.
- The student teacher encourages students' ideas. For example, they might say something like, "That sounds interesting. Can you build on that idea?"
- Students demonstrate respect for the ideas of others, even if they have a different answer, a different approach, or a different perspective.
- Students engage in pair or group conversations in which everyone has an opportunity to contribute to the conversation.
- All students who wish to participate are acknowledged.

If you are submitting an edTPA video and students are rude to the teacher or to each other, or if the teacher is rude to the students on a video clip, that clip will earn a low or failing rubric grade.

Shifting a Classroom's Tone

If you enter a classroom environment that lacks respect, it might be challenging for you to shift the tone in the classroom, but remember that if you strive to build relationships with your students by honoring their interests, backgrounds, and abilities, and consistently demonstrate respect and care to your students, they will reflect that respect back to you.

This kind of a shift is not always instantaneous or consistent, but have faith that you will be able to create respectful relationships and positive interactions with your students. If, however, you have entered a school or classroom with an environment that is pervasively negative and disrespectful, bring that to the attention of your program-based mentors immediately.

RAPPORT

A positive learning environment is a productive classroom in which one can observe an easy, productive flow of conversation and respectful interactions between students and the students and teacher. In this kind of a classroom, the teacher manages the class by effectively employing classroom management strategies, and students demonstrate that they have internalized procedures for managing materials, moving through transitions, sharing ideas with one another, answering questions, and communicating their needs to the teacher.

A positive learning environment is not "ruled by fear," so acting as an authoritarian may keep your students in line, but you want your students to demonstrate that they follow rules because they are interested in the topic and activities, and that they have developed strong, positive relationships with each other and you.

In addition to respectful interactions, you also want to make sure that you demonstrate that you get along with your students and foster an easy flow of conversation. The edTPA calls this "rapport."[1]

What Rapport Looks Like

Rapport looks like a group of students participating in an engaging conversation. They are getting along, the conversation is flowing, and conflict is not present. Everyone is invited and encouraged to participate, and everyone appears to be comfortable and engaged.

Positive rapport can be difficult to establish if a teacher is very strict and students are fearful. In this case, they may participate, but that conversation might be stilted and students may not readily share their interests and questions or elaborate on their ideas or perspectives. Positive rapport can also be difficult to establish if a teacher has weak classroom management skills. In this case, students might interrupt each other, hurt each other's feelings, and exclude others.

PROVIDING STUDENTS WITH APPROPRIATE, LEARNING OBJECTIVE–ALIGNED CHALLENGES

A teacher working in a positive learning environment gives the students a reason to want to participate, a reason to engage. Think of a challenge to engage as an enticing invitation to participate. This is sort of like the "hook" a teacher might use to interest students. This hook might be an intriguing question in which the teacher invites students to speculate about connections between their lives and the topic at hand, or it might be a challenge to solve a problem. It is the kind of invitation that demonstrates to students (and to your evaluator) that you know how to get students excited about learning by connecting the topics or skills you are working with to other topics that you know are important to your students.

Offering challenges like these to students also demonstrates that you are teaching more than just lower-level cognitive functions, such as those lower rungs on Bloom's pyramid.[2] You are not just doing skill work, you are inviting students to engage on those higher-level, more cognitively complex levels.

What Challenge Looks Like

According to clinical mentors, here is what appropriate challenge looks like in a classroom:

- A student teacher poses a complex problem that may have multiple solutions for the students to solve.
- A student teacher asks an open-ended, opinion-based question for the students to deliberate or debate.
- A student teacher wonders what the connection between the topic of study and students' lives outside of school might be.
- The student teacher poses a challenge for the students to attempt, such as building a structure or designing a model.

A Low-Risk Learning Environment

In addition to creating a challenging environment, you also want to establish a low-risk environment where students are not afraid to make mistakes. Watching your students hesitate, make errors, offer incomplete answers/ideas, revise, and rely on others to help them come up with answers/solutions is a positive thing. It means that students are being challenged, but not so much that they don't try.

This means that you are presenting students with several opportunities to engage in higher-order-thinking, again, working at those top levels of Bloom's pyramid, but you have created a low-risk environment where students are not afraid of failing or of being humiliated for attempting something hard.

You want to see students struggling to answer questions or trying challenging activities. However, you want this kind of challenge to happen in a low-risk environment where students are not reprimanded or made fun of when they are not successful, either by other students or by the teacher. You want to create an environment where risk taking, attempting that challenging task, and even failing is rewarded rather than discouraged.

What a Low-Risk Environment Looks Like

- The student teacher asks a challenging question and then supports students by helping them build on each other's ideas toward a possible answer/solution.
- The student teacher offers encouraging words to students when they hesitate. ("Take some time to think about this and don't worry about rushing to answer." Or "If you aren't sure, ask another student.")

- The student teacher models making a mistake and correcting it. The student teacher admits that they do not have the answer to a question and models how to find the answer.

ENGAGING STUDENTS IN
LEARNING OBJECTIVE–ALIGNED ACTIVITIES

Engaging students is crucial. But the engagement needs to be specific. You are not engaging students just to entertain them and make them happy. You want to engage students in activities that they enjoy and that challenge them certainly, but your main objective is to engage students in ways that specifically support their work in the discipline you are teaching and the learning objectives you have established.

So what does this kind of engagement look like? Below are some examples of engaging students in learning based on particular content areas. This section is divided up by discipline so that you can skim through and read about a discipline affiliated with yours. However, it will also be instructive to see what engagement looks like in other disciplines, so reading them all will help you gain a fuller understanding of how you might plan for similar moments.

What Does Engagement Look Like in Literacy?

- Students are having a turn-and-talk conversation about their favorite characters in fairy tales.
- Students are helping the teacher revise a piece of written work by offering suggestions and consulting a revision checklist.
- Students are working together in a small group to complete a graphic organizer in which they identify a text's main ideas and supporting details.

What Does Engagement Look Like in Math?

- The class guides the teacher or another student as they attempt to solve a problem.
- Students discuss the concept that decimals and money are related in a turn-and-talk.
- Students work in pairs, using attribute blocks to build a structure that follows a particular pattern.
- Students work in pairs, taking turns and consulting one another as they work together to solve a quadratic equation.
- Students move throughout the classroom, sketching or taking pictures of particular shapes in a geometry lesson.

What Does Engagement Look Like in ELA?

- In a whole group or small group conversation, students share their understanding of a text.
- Students guide the teacher or another student to identify figurative language in a text.
- Students work in pairs to share and offer revision suggestions using a revision checklist.

What Does Engagement Look Like in Social Studies/History?

- In a whole group or small group conversation, students compare and contrast two historical events.
- Students examine a set of primary source documents and answer questions about them in groups.
- Students engage in a debate in order to understand multiple perspectives on a particular event.

What Does Engagement Look Like in Science?

- Students discuss and answer questions about a text.
- Students engage in a lab/exploration.
- Students work in pairs or guide a teacher/peer to solve an equation.
- Students collaborate in order to build an accurate model.

What Does Engagement Look Like in World Language?

- Students compose a dialogue in which they use a particular set of vocabulary words and write in a particular tense.
- Students guide the teacher or a peer to conjugate a verb in a particular tense.
- Students engage in a turn-and-talk in which they ask and answer questions about a particular topic.

What Does Engagement Look Like in PE?

- Students engage in a drill.
- Students observe each other practice a skill and provide feedback for each other.
- Students engage in an exploration in which a group must work together to meet a goal.
- Students engage in a conversation about strategy.

What Does Engagement Look Like in Health?

- Students work in groups to prepare a PowerPoint presentation to share their understanding of the causes for diabetes type 2.
- Students work as a whole class or in small groups to review food labels and answer questions about a food product's nutritional content.
- Students share graphic organizers that they have filled out in order to share and get feedback on their daily physical activities.

Taking Students' Interests and Experiences into Account when Providing Instruction

When you design a lesson plan, you have an idea of your students' background knowledge, which is comprised of your students' prior knowledge, interests, and the community/culture to which they are connected. As discussed in the previous chapter, you will learn about your students' background knowledge from your cooperating teacher or other school personnel, parents or guardians, assessments you have administered and reviewed, what the students tell you, and of course your own observations.

When you teach your lesson plan, you will want to encourage students to access their background knowledge in order to connect it to the day's learning objectives. So plan to explicitly invite your students to make connections between what they are learning and their background knowledge. Think of this as an invitation you extend to your students to make these connections.

Ideally, you are not just telling students how the new learning will connect to their background knowledge, you are encouraging *them* to make the connections throughout the lesson. You might remind students that they studied a particular topic in a previous unit, or learned particular skills that you will be building on in this unit, and then you might ask students if they can recall what they learned about the topic previously or how to apply a skill or strategy they learned previously that will be useful in the lesson. Then you might ask them to forecast how their prior learning might connect to the new topic.

You might even provide students with an exploration (like a "Do Now") and ask them to share how their background knowledge enabled them to address the question. At the end of a class you might ask students how their learning on this particular day helped them better understand their prior learning or clarify something they learned previously.

What This Looks Like

According to clinical mentors, here are some examples of what inviting students to access background knowledge looks like in a classroom:

- The student teacher reminds students about prior learning and asks students how they might apply that prior learning to a new topic or problem.
- In the context of modeling a skill or working with a topic or text, the student teacher asks the students if this work reminds them of something they have already read or something they have already learned how to do.
- In the context of introducing new content, the student teacher asks students to rely on prior learning to figure out how to understand new content or go about solving a particular problem.
- The student teacher invites students to apply a skill or topic to students' interests or lives outside of school.
- The student teacher asks students why a skill or topic might be important in or outside of school.
- The student teacher makes a reference to students' lives outside of school in the context of working with a topic/skill.
- The student teacher invites students to share connections between the subject and students' interests or backgrounds.

EFFECTIVELY MODELING A SKILL OR STRATEGY

When your instruction is being assessed either on a video or as part of a live observation, you will likely model a skill or strategy that is central to the topic you are teaching and that helps your students meet the learning objective(s) you have articulated in your instructional plan. Modeling affords your students the ability to observe an exemplar so that they understand what their work should look like or include and what criteria are involved in completing a learning task, and it also gives them a chance to ask questions and have them answered.

Modeling usually occurs toward the beginning of a lesson, and often takes the form of a mini-lesson, followed by discussion and then time for students to practice what was just modeled independently.

When you model a skill or strategy, this is an opportunity for you to show your students and your evaluator that you can clearly demonstrate and explain a strategy or procedure, that you can ask a variety of questions of your students in the process, and that you can integrate academic language into your presentation.

Remember that when modeling, you should use a variety of instructional supports, such as demonstrations, both oral and written presentation of directions, and visual representations, such as a graphic organizer or anchor chart. You might also invite students to help you model a procedure or skill while you talk them through the process.

You can also use a model, such as a text or digital technology such as a video or audio recording, to demonstrate a skill or procedure. Students can read, watch, or listen to the model, and then you can facilitate a discussion in which you analyze the resource, discuss what makes it exemplary, how it is constructed, and then connect it to the learning objectives/evaluation criteria you have established.

MANAGING THE LEARNING OF ALL STUDENTS

A college supervisor offers the following observation about managing the learning environment: "Student teachers who demonstrate effective instruction are able to simultaneously support individual students and manage the entire classroom during independent work time."

This statement speaks to a common challenge that candidates confront when they begin leading the whole class for an extended period of time. A candidate is responsible for guiding and managing an entire class of students, but gets easily sidelined by a small group or individual who needs extra attention in the form of extra support or challenge in order to progress and work individually.

The temptation here is to devote time and attention to the student or students who need special attention, but what happens when you do? You lose the rest of the class. When this happens, students who are not being monitored may leave the classroom, get off task and socialize with their peers, or get into trouble. So one has to support students who need extra attention but also monitor the entire class at the same time.

This common challenge requires a candidate to develop their ability to monitor both what is happening right next to them and what is happening on the other side of the classroom, and this takes practice.

One way to help yourself is to think of the classroom as comprised of concentric circles. The candidate has the student(s) who require extra guidance in that circle closest to them but must also be aware of each additional circle radiating from that circle. One needs to be able to attend to the students in that closest circle but also maintain awareness of what is happening in the outer circles as well.

With practice, you will be able to constantly monitor the sounds in the classroom—the entire room all the way out to the outer circle—so you will be able to hear when something sounds "off" even if it is far away from you.

The same ideas applies to seeing in the classroom. It's important to look at the students in your inner circle, but you must also survey the room every few seconds, all the way out to the outer circles. This also takes practice, but if you are aware of the need to monitor all students at all times, and deliberately practice this, you will develop the skill in no time.

The goal is for you to be able to provide guidance to individuals or groups of students and seamlessly manage behavior or provide directions without interrupting the flow of the conversation you are having with a student who needs you.

Some student teachers have found the "ask three and then me" procedure useful when presented with the challenge described above. In most cases, if a student has a question about an instruction in order to get started with independent work, the student can likely find another student who is close by, preferably in the same group, who has the answer. The challenge here is that you don't want students shouting across the room, so they need to ask their group or students sitting next to them.

Another helpful procedure is "wait three and then ask me," which requires students to independently attempt to work out a solution, such as reading the instructions, and then ask the teacher if they cannot continue to work independently after three minutes. This procedure can be highly effective in fostering independence and helping you manage independent work, but you must be consistent in your practice and not deviate from it.

However, the most important strategy you can employ is to *prevent student confusion from the beginning*. That takes preparation. You must anticipate misunderstandings or confusions and ask questions that you have revised so that you know that what you are asking is clearly conveyed. You will want to put strong supports or additional challenges in place by differentiating your instructions and the individual activities for specific students or groups of students. As you gain experience and get to know your students, your cooperating teacher is the best source to help you predict in advance where misunderstandings will occur.

DIFFERENTIATING INSTRUCTION

Just because you have a lesson plan does not mean you will actually implement that plan just as you wrote it. At some point in your teaching, a student will need additional support because the student is confused about how to start independent work or misunderstands a word or instruction. You might also have students who find the work too easy and get bored.

These moments can happen to anyone regardless of their experience, and when they do, they can throw a teacher off course. And though you cannot fully anticipate who will need what supports or challenges at what particular moment each time you teach, your goal should be to anticipate the additional supports and challenges you will need to implement for specific individuals or groups of students so that you minimize these frustrating moments.

You will compose your strategies for differentiation when you write your lesson plans so that when you teach, you will have already made a plan to provide the supports and challenges you anticipate certain groups and individual students will need in your class. Chapters 4 and 5 offer resources to support your efforts to differentiate your instruction for your students. Your cooperating teacher will also be a helpful resource for you because he or she likely knows the students well and has experience successfully supporting and challenging students in the classroom.

What you want to avoid is making your differentiation plan one that you just implement "on the spot" without preplanning, and simply circulating to see "who needs help." That is not a plan. That is a recipe for chaos. If that is your only idea about how to differentiate your instruction, a lot of students will need help because you have not put the proper supports in place for them. Some will be confused and unable to start, and some will finish the independent work so quickly that they will get bored.

There will, without a doubt, be moments in your instruction where you miss an opportunity to support or challenge a student or group of students. This is the nature of teaching. However, the more you *reflect* back on those moments where you missed opportunities in your planning and implementation to provide high-quality supports or challenges for particular students, the better you will get at anticipating student needs, and you will have fewer of those moments.

OFFERING STUDENTS CHOICE

When you differentiate, you have already made the choice in advance about how particular students in your class will interact with the materials and learning activities. Beyond differentiating your materials and the delivery of your instruction, the ability to offer your students some choice about how to engage in a learning activity is a sophisticated teaching skill that you will want to incorporate into your instruction.

Student choice is about having some options built into the lesson plan. For example, if your students are practicing a writing skill such as using dialogue, you might give them a choice about the topic they will write about or maybe even the genre. In a case such as this, you might plan the opportunity for choice in advance of your teaching.

However, there might be some opportunities to give students choice that you don't necessarily plan for. For example, in a lesson on measurement, you might have a student ask if they can approach an assignment in a novel way, such as using a piece of string rather than a ruler to measure an object. If the new approach will help the student meet your learning objective and is not disruptive or overly time consuming, consider allowing it.

Students will frequently offer ideas that can improve the quality of their learning experiences, so be open and invite choice when appropriate. There is something wonderfully democratic about inviting students to bring their interests and talents into the learning activities when possible by letting them offer suggestions about how to approach the topic.

However, not all students and not all student teachers feel comfortable with choice, so you must gauge your teaching and learning context. It is always challenging to figure out how much choice to offer students, no matter how long you have been teaching. Choice is a balancing act. If, for example, you offer too many options or your assignment is too open-ended, that can overwhelm students.

DEEPENING STUDENT LEARNING WITH HIGHER-ORDER-THINKING QUESTIONS

A college supervisor observed, "Student teachers who ask higher-order-thinking questions and then manage the class discussion so that they can build off of each student response and create a complex and meaningful discussion are effective."

Try to incorporate several higher-order-thinking questions in each lesson to ensure that you are engaging your students with the deep ideas that are often conceptual and get at the heart of the discipline you are teaching. And write student responses on the board using the students' language so that their ideas can also be seen. This will support students to give each other feedback and build on each other's responses.

You have likely had some instruction in your teacher education coursework related to the importance of presenting students with higher-order-thinking questions to grapple with in order to help them develop those important, discipline-specific concepts behind the skill work. And if you use the recommended lesson-plan template in this book, you will design some of these questions and place them in your plan so that you can help students have meaningful discussions about these concepts.

When they are just starting to lead a whole class, student teachers often express concern about how to manage class discussions, because they can be unpredictable. What if students don't know how to answer the questions I ask? What if an answer is straight-up wrong? What if a student asks me a question during a discussion, and I don't know the answer? When considering these questions, you can understand why it seems easier and "safer" to simply present information from a PowerPoint without having a discussion.

Yet even if you do engage in direct instruction, it is still crucial to encourage your students to pause and discuss the information being presented. One way to accomplish this is to plan to ask the higher-order-thinking questions throughout your lesson. These are the questions that you will want to include in your lesson plan and revise a few times before you present them to students so that the students clearly understand what is being asked of them.

It does take practice to work effectively with the responses you will receive when you pose a higher-order-thinking question, but work intentionally toward the goal of listening closely to what each student shares with you. Then highlight a shared idea that connects to the question you are asking. Once you highlight that idea, invite someone to build on that idea. If someone provides you with a response that is completely wrong, thank the student for participating, and then ask your class to comment on the part of their response that needs to be refined or corrected. Or thank the student and ask if anyone else has a response and, if that is correct, build on that response.

If several students share responses that are inaccurate, that is a good indication that you need to pause and revisit the topic that is causing them confusion. Remember, those discussions are formative assessments if you are listening for evidence of learning and revising your instruction if necessary.

But the best way to prevent these sorts of awkward moments during discussions is to invite your students to "rehearse" their responses in writing or in a think-pair-share/turn-and-talk activity. That way students will have a chance to have a confusion or misconception corrected by a peer. And if you circulate and listen to student responses, you will know if there are major confusions that you need to refine or interesting responses you want to highlight when you move into a whole-class discussion.

Facilitating Conversations

Sometimes you will structure conversations such as those that may happen in small groups or a turn-and-talk. You will provide students with the questions, you will discuss the roles that each student will play in the partnership or group, and you will establish norms to ensure that the discussions stay on track, involve everyone in the group or pairing, and make certain that students treat one another well and have some accountability about sharing their ideas/progress.

Until you have established the norms for whole-group discussions, as well as a positive and productive learning environment to such an extent that your students can actually facilitate a whole-group discussion, you will facilitate the discussion.

The biggest challenges related to facilitating the discussion of higher-order-thinking questions in a whole group are: (1) asking clear questions that will help students consider content in the way you hope they will; (2) acknowledging student responses; and (3) building on those responses and keeping the conversation going.

Leading discussions takes practice, and it requires that you intentionally write and revise the questions you plan to ask in advance of teaching and that you really listen to what your students are communicating during a class discussion. When you wrote your first lesson plan, you may have written "Then the teacher will ask discussion questions" and not actually composed the questions that you would ask if you were teaching a real lesson.

Student teachers generally learn the importance of not just writing their discussion questions in advance but revising them to make sure that the questions are clear and students will know how to address them.

Try to imagine a moment when you present your students with a higher-order-thinking question and then you realize that the question is too difficult, so they are silent, or too easy, and they answer the question but seem disengaged or bored. How might you handle that so that you can keep your class on track? Or think of those times when you ask a question and a student presents you with a response that is incorrect. What will you do?

REFLECTING ON THE CHAPTER

Effective teachers intentionally design classrooms that are positive learning environments. These classrooms include a range of instructional methods, from direct instruction to project-based learning, but regardless of the particular approach being used, positive learning environments offer learning opportunities to students that are exciting, connected to their backgrounds and interests, accessible to everyone, and appropriately challenging.

Students enjoy exploring big ideas and discussing higher-order-thinking questions that help them work together to come up with answers and ideas as they grapple with the interesting questions at the heart of the disciplines. But as you are learning, this rarely happens by accident, especially when you start teaching. It is all intentionally planned. So how will you work with all of the elements presented in this chapter to design your positive learning environment?

NOTES

1. Board of Trustees of the Leland Stanford Junior University (2018).
2. B. S. Bloom, *Taxonomy of Educational Objectives, Handbook I: The Cognitive Domain* (New York: David McKay, 1956).

Chapter Seven

Analyzing and Acting on Assessment Data

Designing your instruction and assessments, as well as your instructional moves, is important in order to run a successful classroom. But how does a teacher really know if they are doing a good job, and if those plans are coming to fruition in all the ways that they hope and plan they will?

You might assume that a class went well because your students behaved well and seemed engaged in the work. And maybe you even asked them, "Do you understand? Was that clear?" And they might nod their heads or give you a thumbs-up with smiles on their faces. Sometimes students are afraid to admit that they don't understand, sometimes they think that they understand when they don't, and sometimes they just want to please you, so they pretend.

And then . . . you might discover when you ask them probing questions, ask them to summarize what they learned, or give them a quiz that they did not learn what you thought you taught them.

A scenario like that is a common one, and it underscores how crucial it is to also include effective assessment methods in your teaching designs. Chapter 4 will help you plan a variety of assessments, and this chapter provides guidance on how to describe, analyze, and interpret student performance to determine student learning.

This chapter also describes some other important goals of assessment, including communicating your observations to students with thoughtful, aligned feedback (so that students can gain insight into their learning and set goals for themselves as learners) and using assessment data to devise your plans for future learning.

This chapter will also support your work with assessment analysis. You may have to complete an assessment analysis for your student teaching seminar; or if you are preparing an edTPA portfolio, this chapter parallels the Task 3 requirements,[1] which are focused on your work with one assessment.

Sometimes your cooperating teacher reviews assessment data to determine how to group students, to establish what individuals or groups know and don't know, to figure out what they can do or can't do, and to assess how well individuals or groups are progressing. When student teaching, you will observe and participate in a variety of activities centered around assessment data.

As a student teacher, you will not be the primary decision-maker about what assessment tools will be implemented and which ones will be used to generate data for analysis. However, do try to participate in assessment activities with your cooperating teacher whenever possible, because this is an important skill set that you will need when teaching.

In the pages that follow, you will be guided to design evaluation criteria for a summative assessment and to analyze such an assessment so that you can practice creating assessment data to determine student learning and communicate progress to your students.

DEFINING YOUR EVALUATION CRITERIA

Regardless of the type of assessment you administer, and whether it is a pre-assessment, formative assessment, or summative assessment, you must have a crystal clear vision of what you are looking for when you review your students' performance on the assessment. That vision is expressed as your *evaluation criteria*, and whether you engage in an extensive analysis like the one that will be described in this chapter or you do a quick observation during a formative assessment, you will need to consider each assessment with your *evaluation criteria* in mind.

Pre-Assessment

If you are administering a pre-assessment to determine your students' prior learning, you will not just look for prior learning in general. You will look for evidence of the skills and understandings that align with your stated learning objectives, so you have particular evaluation criteria in mind.

Margot's Story

Margot was planning to teach a unit on equivalent fractions to fifth grade students. The learning objective for her first lesson was for students to be able to create equivalent fractions so that they could easily add fractions with like denominators. Margot's cooperating teacher assured her that the students had their multiplication facts down and that they understood what fractions were.

That was a good start, but Margot wanted more information. She administered a pre-assessment to confirm that the class knew their multiplication facts. She also confirmed that the class understood the concept of fractions—they could explain what a numerator conveys and what a denominator conveys.

In addition, Margot wanted to know the extent to which her students grasped the concept of equivalence in fractions. The pre-assessment revealed that, as a group, they did not demonstrate a strong understanding of this concept, so Margot's first lesson plan was designed to help them understand equivalence in fractions.

In this case, Margot's evaluation criteria for the pre-assessment were to (1) determine the extent to which students could solve multiplication problems; (2) determine the extent to which students could explain the concept of a fraction, including the roles of both the numerator and the denominator; and (3) determine the extent to which students could explain whether or not fractions are equivalent. Once Margot had confirmed her students' prior learning, she could establish clear learning objectives for her unit.

Formative Assessment

If you are implementing a formative assessment, even though it is informal, you will not simply be collecting random assessment data. You will look for particular information that you have articulated as your *evaluation criteria*. You will strive to always examine student work to discover the extent to which your students are successfully meeting your designated evaluation criteria, and once you have evidence about how your whole class, groups of students, and individuals are progressing, you can determine whether or not you should move on or circle back and reteach a skill or a concept.

In Margot's case, to teach the concept of equivalent fractions, she modeled equivalent fractions with fraction strips and had students work with fraction strips to build equivalent fractions. Using a formative assessment in which students built equivalent fractions with their fraction strips, Margot was able to determine that most of her students grasped the concept of equivalent fractions, so she moved on to the next part of her lesson, in which she modeled how to create math addition problems based on what students had built with their fraction strips.

You will not likely collect every formative assessment and record it (especially if you are using discussion questions or observations as a formative assessment). However, you will listen to and observe your students in a very targeted way, just like Margot, who was circulating through the classroom and observing to see if students could demonstrate that they were able to build equivalent fractions with their fraction strips.

Margot used a checklist on a clipboard and recorded how many accurate problems each student was able to write. Toward the end of her lesson, Margot used an exit ticket and asked students to describe what they understood from the day's lesson and what was still confusing. When twenty-five out of twenty-nine students wrote that they were not sure how to write math problems to represent what they had built with fraction strips, Margot used her targeted observation recorded on a checklist to corroborate what students self-reported. Then Margot acted on that information and designed a lesson plan to reteach that particular skill/understanding the following day.

Summative Assessment

When reviewing how your students perform on a summative assessment, your method will be more formal and more structured than with a formative assessment. With a formative assessment, you are looking for evidence of student learning over time, and you might be considering only one evaluation criteria at a time. With a summative assessment, you will be looking at the bigger picture, evaluating how students addressed all or most of your unit's evaluation criteria on one assessment. One does not just randomly observe a formative assessment, nor does one randomly score a summative assessment. The teacher is looking for specific evidence of learning.

In regard to the summative assessment's evaluation criteria, it is crucial that *your evaluation criteria be established before you score your students' summative assessments. The evaluation criteria represent the goals you are working toward, and you must clearly communicate these to your students.*

Your evaluation criteria, like other elements of your instructional plans, must align with your central focus, your learning objectives, your disciplinary requirements, and the associated state/national standards you are working with.

Consider your evaluation criteria as a mirror of your learning objectives. You identify clear learning objectives when planning, and you can flip those and use them as your evaluation criteria when assessing.

To illustrate how a teacher identifies the evaluation criteria for a unit and creates a rubric as an assessment tool, consider Daniel's example.

Daniel's Example

Daniel's example comes from his work in an elementary literacy class. Regardless of the grade level or discipline in which you are working, Daniel's analysis provides a strong example of how a student teacher might interpret and consider ways to act on the assessment data they collect and analyze, so as you read, imagine how you might do similar work with your learning objectives and your discipline.

Daniel, a student teacher working in a third grade classroom and reading the story *Charlie* with his students, designed a unit around the following central focus: "Using textual evidence to support their ideas, students will be able to describe a main character from *Charlie* and how that character's actions influenced the plot of the story."

Daniel then identified several learning objectives for the mini-unit/learning segment. They included:

1. Students will be able to describe a character using character traits;
2. Students will be able to identify a character's motivation;
3. Students will be able to use text-based evidence to support the character description;
4. Students will be able to write about the character's actions; and
5. Students will be able to explain how the character's actions contribute to the story's plot.

After working toward each of these objectives in a series of lessons, using formative assessments along the way to ensure that his students were making progress toward the learning objectives, and implementing instructional activities designed to help each student accomplish the objectives, Daniel designed a summative assessment to evaluate each student's learning of all the stated learning objectives. He flipped the learning objectives and rewrote them as the evaluation criteria for the unit's summative assessment. Then he created a rubric comprised of these evaluation criteria.

Because he wanted to ensure that his students understood the evaluation criteria and the descriptions, he revised his learning objectives and made them "I" statements. Daniel made sure to review the rubrics with the students *before* assigning the response.

IDENTIFYING THE EVALUATION CRITERIA

Only include evaluation criteria that you have established as your learning goals. If you expect your students to capitalize proper adjectives correctly or include units of measurement in their answers, establish these as learning objectives/evaluation criteria and review the topics with your students. If you expect students to edit their work, review that topic with them and provide them a checklist or some pointers. If you expect your students to use specific academic vocabulary, make your expectations clear and review the vocabulary with them.

Table 7.1.

Evaluation Criteria	Effective 3	Developing 2	Ineffective 1
I described a character using character traits.	Description has more than three character traits, both internal and external.	Description has at least three character traits.	Description has fewer than three character traits, and/or traits are not accurate.
I described a character's motivation.	Well-described motivation and accurate to the story.	An accurate description of one character's motivation.	Not well described and/or inaccurate to the story.
I used text-based evidence to support my ideas.	More than three examples of evidence to support ideas. The evidence clearly supports ideas.	At least three examples of text evidence to support ideas. The evidence matches ideas.	Few examples of text evidence to support ideas, or the evidence does not match ideas.
I described the character's actions.	A clear and detailed description of the character's actions.	A clear description of the character's actions.	A vague or inaccurate description of the character's actions.
I wrote about the importance of a character's actions to the overall plot of the text.	A clear and detailed statement about how the character's actions contribute to the plot.	A clear statement about how the character's actions contribute to the plot.	A vague or inaccurate statement about how the character's actions influenced the overall plot.

Including criteria on a rubric that were not identified and acted on as learning objectives is unfair and confusing to students and misaligned with your other planning elements.

Working with Prepublished Rubrics

If you are using a prepublished rubric that is part of your curriculum or that you found online, that is fine as long as the evaluation criteria match up with your learning objectives. If not, you must modify the rubric so that it matches your learning objectives (just make sure you cite the source).

ANALYZING ASSESSMENT RESULTS FOR YOUR WHOLE CLASS

Once Daniel read the papers and scored them using the rubric, he didn't just return the scores to students, write the scores in his gradebook, and move on to the next topic. He spent some time analyzing his assessment results. In order to do that in a systematic way, Daniel created a table that documented how each student did on each criterion of the summative assessment.

Daniel also created a row at the bottom of the table where he recorded his class averages *for each evaluation criterion* and also for the total points. This made it easy for him to understand the extent to which his students were able to demonstrate growth overall *but also with regard to each specific evaluation criterion* (learning objective).

When you review table 7.2, consider how much information the table provides about how the students performed on the summative assessment. If Daniel simply recorded each student's score in a gradebook, he would have some information about student performance but not the detailed breakdown for each evaluation criterion demonstrated above. The more detailed your breakdown, the more thorough your analysis.

ANALYZING AND REFLECTING ON YOUR RESULTS

Once you have built your evaluation criteria, administered your summative assessment, scored your rubrics, and charted out the scores for all students as described above, you will analyze your results.

Table 7.2.

Students	I described a character by using character traits	I described a character's motivation	I used text-based evidence to support my response	I described my character's actions	I wrote about the importance of a character's actions to the overall plot of the text	Score
Student 1	1	3	3	3	3	3
Student 2	1	2	2	2	2	2
Student 3	2	1	3	2	1	2
Student 4	1	2	2	2	2	2
Student 5	1	2	3	2	2	2
Student 6	1	2	3	1	3	2
Student 7	2	1	2	2	3	2
Student 8	1	2	2	2	2	2
Student 9	1	3	1	3	2	2
Student 10	1	2	2	1	3	1
Student 11	2	1	2	2	2	2
Student 12	3	2	3	3	3	3
Student 13	2	2	2	2	3	2
Student 14	3	1	2	3	2	2
Student 15	2	2	2	2	2	2
Student 16	2	1	2	2	3	2
Student 17	3	1	3	1	3	2
Student 18	1	3	2	1	2	2
Student 19	2	1	1	2	3	2
Student 20	1	2	3	1	3	2
Student 21	3	1	3	2	2	2
Class Average	1	2	2	2	3	2

A good place to start with analysis is to think about a few questions you want to answer when you examine your assessment data. The following list can be used to help you make sense of that data:

1. What patterns do I see when I examine the whole group's performance? As a group, on what evaluation criteria did the class do well, and where did the students struggle?
2. What patterns do I see when I examine the performance of specific groups of students? For example, are there any trends among my emergent bilingual students? Are there any trends among my struggling readers? What do I notice about the performance of those students who struggle to recall math facts?
3. Then examine the performance of some individual students, such as those who are outliers (meaning that their performance on the assessment was quite different than the average) or those with special learning needs.

You might also spend some time considering the performance of an individual who is doing "fine" in order to better learn how they are thinking about and working with the assessment material. Often students who are doing "just fine" get neglected in favor of those outliers.

Analyzing your assessment data with these questions in mind will help you figure out what kind of general feedback to provide groups and individual students, what kind of remediation or challenges you need to implement for the group or individuals going forward, and what kinds of misunderstandings you can anticipate from the group or individuals in the future.

Teachers can analyze and reflect on their assessment results in order to understand how and why students performed as they did, and this will help you provide targeted feedback and determine how best to build on what they were able to do or remediate.

The more detailed and specific you can be in your analysis, the better you will get at analyzing student work.

BENCHMARKS

The term "benchmark" usually refers to a particular assessment, such as a "benchmark exam," which measures the extent to which a student is proficient in a number of areas. Teachers also use this term to mean a standard (such as a percentage score) that indicates proficiency and, therefore, reveals to the teacher that the student has learned the idea/skill/procedure so that they can move on and build on that learning.

You should ask your cooperating teacher if there is generally a class average earned by the whole class that indicates the teacher can move on. Many teachers consider an average of 80 percent to be mastery, for example. So for the assessment above, if Daniel is looking at an average of 80 percent to indicate that he can move on, the teacher may want to add another lesson to reteach all of the criteria or some of the criteria where the students generally scored the lowest (such as writing about character traits, which had a class average of 1).

FIGURING OUT WHAT TO DO WITH YOUR ASSESSMENT RESULTS

Moving on to Your Next Steps

Once your students (or a group or an individual) demonstrate that they have sufficiently met the learning objectives assessed, you can consider those learning objectives prior learning so when you think about what comes next, after a summative assessment, you will be building on that prior learning. The edTPA uses the term "next steps" to identify the informed (by the assessment results) actions the teacher will take to support his/her/their students to now apply this prior learning to a new or more complex topic or task.

For example, if your students demonstrate that they can apply a reading strategy to a text, then the next step might be that they will apply the reading strategy to a more complex text.

If your students demonstrate that they can identify simile in a series of poems, the next step may be to have them apply their new learning to the composition of their own, original poems in which they use simile effectively.

If your students demonstrate that they have mastered some basketball skills and ball control, could your next step be to design game or competitive drills and work with your students to consider the strategic application of their newly learned skills?

Because you will likely be student teaching in a classroom with a curriculum that has already been established in a textbook or a predetermined unit, notice that the new learning opportunities will build on the learning your students demonstrated in the previous unit. A cohesive curriculum is constructed in that manner, logically building student knowledge and skills.

If the "next steps" can be accomplished when working on a new unit/learning segment, such as the study of a new, more complex text, then you know to move on. And even though not all students will meet your benchmark on every criterion, you can deliberately target students who did not meet those benchmarks and intentionally design activities to help support their development even while moving on to a new text.

In addition, you can also devise ways to challenge your students who met the benchmarks so that they are also continually progressing. You will certainly have some students who worked through a previous unit easily and require extra challenge regarding your learning objectives, so you will want to take that information into the next steps you design for them.

WHAT HAPPENS WHEN STUDENTS DO NOT MEET THE LEARNING OBJECTIVES?

One of the greatest challenges for teachers is considering what to do when they administer an assessment and find that not every student has demonstrated that they have met the benchmark for every evaluation criterion. What can a teacher do if he/she/they planned to move on, building on the knowledge and skills just assessed, but not every student is there yet?

In this case it will be necessary to engage those students who need some remediation in reteach activities. A reteach ("reengagement" is another term) can happen in the classroom context during study time or choice time in an elementary context and in study hall or after school in a secondary context.

You might also look ahead to your future curriculum and revise it, devising opportunities to circle back to the ideas/skills/procedures for which some students may need continued support, even as you move on to more advanced work. This method is central to a spiral curriculum[2] in which, though the instruction moves on to address new topics, the teacher often returns to previously taught topics in order to reinforce the skills or understandings on which the new learning is built.

For example, if you teach math and your students do not have their multiplication facts memorized (which can still be the case in a secondary context), you will need to build some multiplication practice into your regular math classes. You might engage the class in a game or have them complete "Mad Minutes."

In ELA, you might work with story elements over the course of an academic year, working to identify and develop an understanding of how plot, character, setting, and theme interact in a text. You will spiral back to build the skills of identifying story elements and describing how they contribute to an understanding of a text, even while you introduce increasingly complex texts.

In a physical education setting, you may move your students into competitive play during a basketball unit, but you will periodically return to the topic of dribbling cues in order to give students the opportunity to refine the skill of dribbling.

In a social studies context, you might work with students to continually refine their abilities to work with questions that help them analyze primary source documents from multiple perspectives, even as you present increasingly challenging material.

A reteach does not need to take an entire period, but providing some extra work to continue to hone those skills allows you to move on while reinforcing and improving previously taught skills.

Remember that if the class, groups of students, or one student did not meet the learning objective the first time you assessed them, either informally (formative assessment) or formally (summative assessment), you will want to devise a different way of presenting that skill/strategy/understanding rather than simply repeating what you just did in a reteach.

For example, you might employ a different modality—such as a visual component—or you might build in extra steps by breaking the learning demand down more. You could also add supports such as a vocabulary list, the use of manipulatives, or other hands-on resources.

If your class, groups of students, or one individual struggled to demonstrate conceptual understanding in math, what else could you do to help them successfully demonstrate conceptual understanding? Maybe they need more support with the vocabulary to express the concept, or perhaps they need more hands-on work with manipulatives in order to grasp the concept.

You may have one or two students who struggled with some of the learning objectives/evaluation criteria, but they may have struggled in different ways, so their next steps might include supports that are different. One may require some language support, and one may require you to break a procedure down into smaller steps.

You will know precisely where these struggles are because, like Daniel, you will have analyzed in detail the new learning they were able to demonstrate and where they fell short on their summative assessments. Again, that is the value of having very specific evaluation criteria on your table.

Pacing

Interview any practicing student teacher and you will learn that the academic schedule rarely permits the teacher's desired time to reteach skills and understandings before moving on. This is a less-than-ideal situation and can be quite frustrating, but it is a very realistic one that student teachers encounter, as the teaching schedule, which includes pacing guidelines, is often created before the start of the school year and may be influenced by a prepackaged curriculum or by a testing schedule, so you may not have much choice about what to teach next.

Because prepackaged curriculum programs are not designed for the particular students in any given classroom, student teachers who are working closely with their students often, correctly, feel as if the class is being "rushed" to cover material.

Though it is not responsible to move on to a new topic of study if the majority of the class has not met whatever benchmarks have been established to demonstrate that the majority of the class has learned the material, teachers are sometimes under intense pressure to continue moving through curriculum, and they don't always take the time to ensure that everyone is ready to move on. That doesn't mean that the teacher is a bad teacher, but there may be outside influences directing pacing.

If you have questions about pacing and how the cooperating teacher has made the decision to move on to a new topic of study, ask and find out. You will likely learn a great deal about how decisions about curriculum and pacing are made. Once you understand how external forces can influence the extent to which you can move on and devise "next steps," you will be able to identify spaces where you can customize instruction, circling back to reteach or challenge as needed. You may never feel completely satisfied that you have met the needs of each student 100 percent, but do work with the intention to do so.

THE IMPORTANCE OF FEEDBACK

Reflect on how often in your own academic life you have received feedback with a letter grade, paused to look at the grade, and then turned your attention elsewhere, not really looking at the comments on your returned assessment.

Because school life is fast-paced, the inclination is to move on to the next activity or learning opportunity. As a result, we rarely make the time to consider the feedback we have received or to give students enough time to process that feedback before we move on. This is especially true if the feedback is delivered long after an assignment has been completed and is no longer considered relevant by the students, or if the feedback is cursory and not really aligned with the goals of the assignment.

The job of assessment is not just about evaluating student learning, it is also about communicating effectively with students about their progress so that each student has a clear understanding of what they are doing well, where they need to improve, and HOW to improve.

Making Sense of Feedback

Using an assessment tool (such as a rubric or checklist) that is shared with students *before* they are sent off to complete an assessment supports students because it clearly breaks the assessment down so that they can see specifically where they are in relation to the learning objectives.

When we consider Daniel's assessment data, it is clear that not all students earn consistent scores on each learning objective—there is variation between students and variation in performance for individuals. With specific feedback, such as a detailed rubric score, each student can examine where they need to improve in order to move up on the rubric scale, and they can also understand their strengths.

As stated earlier in this chapter, it is important to review the rubric or checklist prior to assigning an assessment so that students clearly understand the criteria they are working toward and know how you expect them to demonstrate their learning.

It can also be helpful to offer students an exemplar model, and then have students analyze the model in order to clearly see the evaluation criteria in a completed assignment. This will also support your students' understanding with regard to your feedback, as they have already practiced giving feedback when analyzing the model.

As a student teacher, you might not have models available, so sometimes you need to create them or ask you cooperating teacher if he or she has one. If you teach in a context where the model can be a demonstration of a skill or procedure, that demonstration functions as an exemplar.

Having this understanding will also help your students make sense of the feedback you provide them because it will be aligned with that criteria. You don't want to provide random feedback that does not connect to those goals, because it will not be as impactful or relevant to students. One feedback strategy that student teachers find effective is to provide additional comments with the scored rubric or checklist they return to their students.

Glow and Grow

Take two sticky notes; on one write "glow," and on the other one write "grow." On the "glow" sticky note, write one or two evaluation criteria for which the student demonstrated learning. On the "grow" note, write one or two evaluation criteria that you hope your student will improve on. You can place those on the scored checklist or rubric. That way the student has access to a breakdown of how they did regarding the evaluation criteria as well as your interpretation of their performance on the sticky notes.

Consider Daniel's reflection on the feedback he provided for one of his students:

> For student 14, I wrote a GLOW statement about her areas of strength. This states that she included a strong opening statement by asking the reader a question. I informed the student that this was a powerful way to hook the reader. I also highlighted how she included a character's actions and stated specific instances where she used a character's actions to support the claim: "Jean told Charlie to not banish Suzanne. She affected the story the most because she got shot down."
>
> The GROW statement about areas of improvement noted that the student needs to pay attention to citing text evidence to support or justify her response next time. I provided an example/sentence frame that would guide the student's thinking, "I think Jean affected the story the most because she was Charlie's mother. I know this because in chapter 14 on page 101, the text says . . ."

Make sure that you select and include specific feedback that addresses at least one "glow" and at least one "grow" comment for each student, and align your feedback to your learning objectives/evaluation criteria.

Setting Time Aside for Students to Consider Their Feedback

In addition to providing timely, specific, and aligned feedback that speaks to the strengths and challenges a student demonstrated on an assessment, make a plan to help students consider and use the feedback you provide.

Help Each Student UNDERSTAND and APPLY the Feedback

If we do not structure ways to help students make sense of and actually apply their feedback, it is likely that the feedback gets filed (or thrown) away and forgotten, if it is even read. In that case, time spent writing feedback is wasted. It can be very helpful to have a routine that you establish in your classroom to help students review, understand, and then make a plan to apply the feedback to their future learning. In fact, your cooperating teacher may already have such a routine in place, so it would be wise to ask about this and continue to implement it when you provide feedback.

Thomas's Story

Thomas, an ELA student teacher, used a literary essay as a summative assessment. One student explained their interpretation of the assigned poem well, but the student did not include textual evidence in that interpretation, which was one of the learning objectives for the assessment. Thomas conferenced with the student, guiding her to establish the very specific goal of including at least three pieces of textual evidence in her next literary essay.

The student kept track of that goal in her class notebook, in the section where she listed her ELA goals, and worked toward it on the next essay. Thomas could have also assigned a revision of the original essay, requiring the student to add at least three pieces of text evidence, before moving on.

In this case, Thomas met individually with the student to ensure that the student understood the feedback, helped the student establish a specific goal, and then designed an opportunity for the student to apply the feedback.

Fatema's Story

Fatema, a student teacher working in a secondary science classroom, held a similar conference with a student who had difficulty describing his understanding of how and why a procedure worked during a lab assignment. In this case, the student had not included the assigned science vocabulary in the description, so Fatema demonstrated how to incorporate that vocabulary, therefore making the description clearer. Then Fatema provided the student with the opportunity to revise his response applying the feedback.

Daniel also described how he supported his student to understand and apply the feedback he provided her:

> One way I did support focus student 14 to apply and use the feedback to further her learning related to the learning objectives at a later time was by reviewing the assessment with the student through one-to-one conferencing. Student 14 is approaching grade level in reading. As a result, I asked student 14 to reflect on her work in order to address areas of strengths and weakness. In order to reflect deeply, one question I asked student 14 is, "Can you point to the place in your extended response where you might change it?" Next, I invited the student to set goals. According to her assessment data, student 14 struggled with identifying a character's motivation. To meet her goals, she will consider the following questions the next time she writes a similar piece: "Did I write about a character's motivation? Are my ideas clearly expressed? Did I use text evidence to support my response?"

Advice about Feedback from Former Student Teachers

Below is some advice from student teachers about methods they have successfully used when working with assessment feedback:

- Make sure that feedback is specific and connected to your learning objectives/stated evaluation criteria.

- Use a model to help students locate evaluation criteria in the assignment and provide feedback according to what they observe in the model.
- Have students keep track of the goals they set after considering your feedback. They can use index cards, sticky notes, or a journal where they record and reflect on learning goals.
- Work hard to return student work with feedback soon after it is submitted. That way the feedback will be timely and meaningful.
- Remember that feedback does not have to always be written. Use one-to-one conferences or experiment with audio recordings also.
- Provide time during class for students to process the feedback you have provided—give them time to ask questions about the feedback, reflect on the feedback, and set goals.
- If students have the evaluation criteria in mind before they engage in the assessment, they will know what to focus on and will not be surprised when they receive their feedback.
- Don't overwhelm your students (or yourself) with feedback. It is fine to identify one "glow" and one "grow."
- Give your students plenty of opportunity to provide each other (and you) with feedback. That will help them learn the value of feedback and understand how it connects to specific criteria rather than general praise or criticism.
- When you give students feedback, make sure you give them an opportunity to apply it soon after they receive it so that they don't completely forget.

Again, feedback is a crucial part of assessment and, as a student teacher, you will likely spend a lot of time providing feedback in various ways, but students will not naturally pause and reflect on that feedback. Therefore, teachers need to set up the structures to help them do that and, in doing so, can support their metacognitive practices too. They will learn from us how to reflect on their learning and development so that they can continue to improve.

REFLECTING ON THE CHAPTER

Prior chapters addressed the important elements that make up instructional/assessment design. Equally important is assessment analysis and communicating with students about their learning. If you don't analyze your student learning, you won't have a clear vision about what to teach next. If you don't provide students with thoughtful and aligned feedback, they won't have a clear vision about their progress.

Teaching without assessment analysis is a little like trying to navigate in the dark without GPS. What aspects of assessment analysis seem clear and easy? Which ones seem more complicated? Make sure to interview your cooperating teacher about how they work with assessment analysis, and try to assist by evaluating student work and providing feedback so that you can get a lot of practice.

NOTES

1. Board of Trustees of the Leland Stanford Junior University (2018).
2. Howard Johnston, "The Spiral Curriculum. Research into Practice," Education Partnerships, 2012, https://eric.ed.gov/?id=ED538282.

Chapter Eight

Composing a Strong, Aligned edTPA*

This chapter is written for teacher candidates who are preparing their edTPAs. Building on the guidance offered in earlier chapters, this chapter will provide you with an overview, as well as important tips and checklists created with input from student teachers who earned high scores about their preparations and methods.[1]

WHAT IS THE EDTPA?

"edTPA™ is a performance-based, subject-specific assessment and support system used by more than 600 teacher preparation programs in some 40 states to emphasize, measure and support the skills and knowledge that all teachers need from Day 1 in the classroom."[2]

At this point in your teacher education program, you will know for certain whether your state requires all teacher candidates to take and pass the edTPA in order to become certified. If you are enrolled in a teacher education program, you will likely prepare your edTPA portfolio during student teaching.

This is not an exam that you sit for; rather, it is a portfolio that you build and submit to Pearson, either directly on their website or through software used by your teacher preparation program, such as Chalk & Wire or Tk20.

The edTPA is not cheap. It will cost you $300 to get your exam scored by Pearson. And if you fail one task of this exam, it will cost $100 to resubmit and have the task rescored. If you fail more than one task, you will have to resubmit

---

*The author is not affiliated with Stanford University or its licensee, Pearson. The content in this book is not sponsored or endorsed by Stanford University or Pearson, nor has it been reviewed by Stanford University or Pearson.

and have those tasks rescored. That will cost you another $300. So it is important to prepare your edTPA correctly, ensuring that you only submit it once.

Begin your edTPA preparations with the understanding that this is a time-consuming assessment on which you must spend a significant amount of effort writing, compiling, and organizing your materials, as well as responding to a series of prompts that are provided as templates.

Understand that you will not pass the edTPA by luck, magic, or with wishful thinking. You will need to be very organized about how you approach the edTPA and *work smart*. Though this book is written for all student teachers, whether they must prepare an edTPA or not, the structure, terminology, and the suggestions in this book are aligned with the edTPA in order to support candidates, so reviewing the previous chapters will support your edTPA efforts.

EDTPA: GETTING ORGANIZED CHECKLIST

Because you will be composing and collecting a variety of artifacts, as well as completing templates, you will have to be very organized when preparing your edTPA. Start by reviewing the checklist below to help you get an idea of what you will be doing and to help you keep track of the important actions you will need to take to compile your edTPA.

This checklist conveys the order in which you should accomplish each task. Try to accomplish these objectives in the first few weeks of student teaching. The earlier, the better.

- ☑ Set up one folder titled edTPA, with three subfolders (four for elementary) for each task. Make sure you have a plan to regularly back up your work (or use Google Drive).
- ☑ Ask your college instructor how you will get your handbook and your templates. Do you need to register with Pearson or access them on a platform such as Tk20?
- ☑ Once you have your templates, organize them in the appropriate folder.
- ☑ Read through the descriptions of each task and part in this chapter so that you can gain a general overview of what you will be producing and collecting.
- ☑ Schedule a meeting with your cooperating teacher *in the first week of your placement* to determine the topic for your instructional unit and to decide on the dates when you will teach, record your lesson plans, and administer a summative assessment.[3]
- ☑ Have a conversation with your cooperating teacher and other school personnel in order to better understand your student teaching context.

- ☑ Have a conversation with your cooperating teacher to determine what curriculum you will use for your lesson plans. Will you use a textbook or program for example, or will you use a curriculum that your cooperating teacher wrote? Will you be asked to write your own curriculum from scratch?
- ☑ If you are working in a secondary context, ask your cooperating teacher to help you locate one focus class.
- ☑ If you are working on the special education handbook, ask your cooperating teacher to help you find one student as your focus student.
- ☑ Have a conversation with your cooperating teacher about the specific learning needs and preferences of the students in your class and how they are grouped.
- ☑ Copy and distribute a video permission form to your students. You can get this from your program or ask your cooperating teacher for a district or school form.
- ☑ Draft the central focus for your unit and check with your cooperating teacher to make sure your central focus is realistic for the students in your class.
- ☑ Identify your learning objectives and related standards. Make sure you meet all of the disciplinary requirements in your handbook. These disciplinary requirements will be presented in your handbook. See the references section for a resource to help you with these disciplinary standards.
- ☑ Check with your cooperating teacher to make sure that your learning objectives/standards are on target and to help you locate materials for your lessons, such as texts, videos, artistic supplies, manipulatives, lab supplies, etc.
- ☑ Draft your summative assessment and the evaluation criteria that you will use to evaluate each student's performance on the summative assessment.
- ☑ Check with your cooperating teacher to make sure that the summative assessment and evaluation criteria are realistic, and review any assessment accommodations or modifications that you want to make for specific groups or individuals.
- ☑ Draft your three to five lesson plans. Refer to chapters 4 and 5 to support this work.
- ☑ Check with your cooperating teacher to make sure that your lesson plan drafts are realistic—that you aren't trying to accomplish too much or too little in one class period.
- ☑ Decide what device you will use to record your teaching of the lesson plans. Test out the device to make sure you have enough memory to record about three 45-minute classes, that your volume works, and experiment with camera angles. Also, test your device to make sure you can take your recording off of your device (delete it to save memory) and back it up

on a computer. Figure out how you will make your video clips once you have uploaded them onto a computer. Will you use iMovie or Windows Movie Maker? You won't be able to edit your clips, but you will need to use editing software to pull them out of your recordings as a clip.

☑ Strive to create and collect all of your artifacts in the first part of your student teaching semester. If your semester is divided into two placements, try to have all of your artifacts collected by the seventh week so that you have the next half of student teaching to write your commentaries. Doing so will ease some of your stress about creating and collecting your artifacts.

AN OVERVIEW OF THE TASKS

Before you gather or compose anything for your portfolio, it is important to get a sense of what goes into that portfolio—what will be your key student teaching tasks. This section provides a detailed walk-through of the edTPA and specifically describes what you will need to do and gather in order to get organized and make sure you have the materials you need. It is a good idea to read through this chapter early on in the process so that you have a preview of what you will need, and then return to examine descriptions of tasks when questions arise for you.

TASK 1

Part A—Context for Learning (Template)

This is a template that you will get from your college instructor or directly from Pearson when you register. On this template you will describe your teaching context such as the general type and location of your school, any special features of the community, school, and classroom. You will describe any specific curriculum you use and the pacing in your classroom.

You will also describe any special classroom features and how students are grouped. Finally, you will describe the learners in your classroom. If you have classified students, students with special linguistic needs, struggling or advanced students, or students with particular learning styles that require accommodations or modifications, you will list them. *Make certain that you do not identify your district or school by name and that you do not use the names of students in this template or anywhere in the edTPA.*

Advice

Sometimes teacher candidates wonder whether or not they should leave students with IEPs or English Language Learners off of the chart in this template. Their rationale for this is that, in theory, a candidate can fail a rubric if they indicate that they have special needs in their class but fail to provide the supports/accommodations in their plans and assessments. One answer to this is that, on the edTPA, you want to be honest and accurate and also show off that you can accommodate a variety of learners. Do know that you will score higher on the rubrics if you demonstrate this ability.

Furthermore, in order to use this assessment to improve your knowledge and teaching skills, it's smart to practice differentiating in order to add some more tools to your teaching tool box. So if you have a wide range of learners, demonstrate that you know how to support all of them. You will appreciate this experience when you start teaching.

Part B—Lesson Plans for Learning Segment (Word Document)

You will need to plan a mini-unit/learning segment of three to five lessons. Each lesson plan should be no longer than four pages in length. Identify each plan by day (day 1, day 2, etc.). You should administer a summative assessment at the end of your learning segment, so plan to do so on the last day of that mini-unit. For example, you might write lesson plans for three days and then administer a summative assessment on day 4. Thus, you will need to schedule those four days with your cooperating teacher as soon as possible.

Part C—Instructional Materials (Word Document)

This section of the edTPA is very simple. For each lesson plan you create (each day), you will list the materials you plan to use. Create a Word document and write out what materials you will use in order: "Instructional materials for day 1," etc. You can include books, pages of a book, pictures of anchor charts, PowerPoint slides (just reduce them to fit them on a page), technology that you use, a description of manipulates that you use, lab equipment, sports equipment, and any other materials that you plan to use during instruction.

Part D—Assessments (Word Document)

In this section you will list (and include blank copies of) all of your assessments. You will create a Word document for this part. Write out your assessments in order: "Assessments for day 1, day 2," etc. Include *all* assessments, even formative assessments, such as questions you plan to ask and possible answers and turn-and-talks and possible responses. If you differentiate any assessment, make sure you include the differentiated versions. You will include your summative assessment (and any differentiated versions of it) here as well. Again, all of the assessments you include in this part are blank.

It is a good idea to use the table in chapter 4 of this book to help you organize your assessments by day. You might place that table at the top of this Word document and then include the actual blank assessments underneath.

Part E—Planning Commentary (Template)

Just like Task 1A, this is a template that you will get from your college instructor or directly from Pearson when you register. On this template, you will respond to several prompts. If you review chapter 4 and address the topics on the provided lesson-plan template, you will be well set up to address the prompts.

You will be required to describe your central focus for the learning segment as well as your learning objectives and standards. You will be asked to describe your disciplinary standards as well. See the references section for a resource to help you with these disciplinary standards.

You will also be required to describe how you plan to address the academic language that connects to your central focus. See chapter 4 for a discussion of academic language and the references section for some resources to help you with academic language. You will be required to describe the assessments you have planned and how you will differentiate the assessments to support all of the students in your class. Again, reference the assessment table that you create when you respond to this question.

TASK 2

Part A—Video Clip(s)

Here you will submit a video clip or two for your scorer to review. You can submit one clip (most handbooks require less than 20 minutes, but some require just 15, so check your handbook).

It is recommended that you submit two clips that total your allotted time. For example, if you can submit 20 minutes of teaching footage, submit two clips that together total 20 minutes, such as 7 minutes and 13 minutes, 5 and 15, 10 and 10, etc.

When you submit these clips, they must be compressed. YouTube is the best place for you to find out how to compress your video clips given the type of camera/computer you are using. Make certain that your clips are not edited. They must be continuous.

It is a good idea to record ALL of your lesson plans, and not just one day's plan. You never know what may go wrong during your lesson or if you will have technical troubles with your recording.

Also, having all of your lesson plans recorded gives you plenty of footage to choose from and ensures that you will have everything you need to address the prompts in Part B. Note that you can also use videos in Task 3 as evidence, so the more footage you have, the better.

Part B—Instruction Commentary (Template)

This is a template that, just like the Task 1 templates, you will get from your college instructor or directly from Pearson when you register. On this template you will address questions that ask you to describe the instruction that will be viewed on the video recording. *It is very important that you review the prompts you will be asked about your recording before you create your lesson plans.*

You will be asked to address how your pedagogy addresses specific questions. Review chapter 6 to help you address the prompts on this template.

Know that your scorer will be looking at your video for evidence of specific instructional practices, and you will need to point to moments in your video clip as evidence that you did work with these.

Selecting Your Video Clips

It's a violation of the edTPA "Guidelines for Acceptable Candidate Support"[4] for your mentors to review your video and tell you what clips to use. However, if you review the prompts you must address in Task 2 prior to writing your lesson plans, as described in chapter 3, you will know how to set up the moments you will need to reference as evidence for the assertions you will make in response to the Task 2 prompts.

After you have taught and recorded your lessons, review those Task 2 prompts again before you select your clips. The prompts can guide you as you select your clips, because you will naturally want to select video that addresses those questions.

Include Time Stamps When You Write Your Commentary

When writing Task 2, you cannot just claim that you did, at some vague point, meet a prompt's requirements; you must prove it with evidence, and your evidence must be time stamped in your recordings. When you write your commentary, include your time stamps just as you would cite a quote or specific example in an essay.

Here is an example:

> I have created a positive learning environment in my classroom, as evidenced by the fact that I warmly greet my students when they enter the classroom (Clip 1: 2 minutes, 16 seconds); I thank them, using their names when they respond to a question (Clip 1: 4 minutes, 12 seconds; Clip 2: 3 minutes, 23 seconds); they engage in respectful conversations with each other (Clip 2: 5 minutes, 33 seconds; Clip 2: 6 minutes, 42 seconds); and they remain respectful to each other, even when they disagree, as they did when the student in the blue shirt offered an alternative solution to the one shared by the student in the yellow shirt (Clip 1: 7 minutes, 54 seconds).

You can use the same time stamp (moment from a clip) to address multiple questions. For example, you might use a class discussion to demonstrate a positive learning environment and also deepening content understanding.

Experiment with Your Technology Early

Experiment with your recording technology prior to recording your lessons so that you ensure that you know how to use it, know how to turn the volume on, have plenty of memory to record, and have selected camera angles that capture you and the students from whom you have permission. The person recording you can walk around with the recorder and move; the recording does not need to be stationery.

Permission Slips

Don't record your video until you have collected your permission slips, and make certain that you show only those students for whom you have permissions in your video. Students who did not return permission slips can be placed in the back of the classroom or off to the sides to make recording easier. Translate your permission slips if needed so that they are accessible to all of your students' parents.

Do Not Edit Your Videos, Even by Accident

You will likely have your cooperating teacher, other school personnel, or maybe even a student teacher also working in your building record your lessons. Make sure that you instruct them not to stop the recording FOR ANY REASON. If the recording is stopped and then started again, edTPA considers that to be editing.

Consider Peter's Story

Peter, a secondary math candidate, once had his Task 2 returned unscored from Pearson and was told that his clips were edited. He didn't know why. Peter sent them to his college mentor to review, and he couldn't figure out why either.

However, when Peter watched the videos a second time, he noticed that the clips he submitted had stopped and started again numerous times. Those stops and starts were very subtle and not noticeable at first, but Pearson noticed it. And, as it turns out, Peter's cooperating teacher had kept starting and stopping the recording to try and avoid recording a student who was acting out. The problem with this is that Peter did not notice the stops and starts because they happened so quickly.

Unfortunately, a large section of his recording could not be used because of the stopping and starting. Peter missed out on using a potentially strong clip. Student teaching had ended and it was summer when he noticed this, so he had to use another clip from his recording on a different day and rewrite his entire Task 2 to fit his new clip. However, Peter was glad that he recorded all three of his lessons. Otherwise, he would have had to figure out how to get back into the school and reteach.

Planning Your Clips

You'll want to check your handbook to see how best to set up your clips, but in general, you want your first clip to show you instructing your whole group. (Most handbooks consider a group of four students to be a class.) You should be leading a discussion in which you and your students are working with academic language where you are modeling a skill/understanding related to your central focus, posing and discussing higher-order-thinking questions, and eliciting and building on student responses to address those higher-order-thinking questions.

You should be using modeling, demonstrations, representations, anchor charts, and instructions in this clip. If you have structured your lesson plans so that they follow a "gradual release of responsibility" model, this would likely be the first part of your lesson or the "I do/we do" progression.

Your second clip should be of you supporting your students while they attempt to apply the skill/procedure/understanding that you modeled in the first clip. You do not want to use a clip of students just working quietly or in groups; make sure that you are present and involved by asking questions, providing support, and giving high-quality, aligned feedback.

Academic Language

Even though you won't have a specific academic language question in Task 2, when you write Task 3 (for most handbooks), you will be asked to assess how well your students worked with the academic language you planned for in your lesson plans.

You can certainly point to the summative assessments to address this, but you also have the option to pull evidence from the clips you upload for Task 2. Therefore, you might want to give yourself some room to work with academic language. You will certainly introduce the language demands in your first clip, and you will set up, provide feedback for, and generally support students to use the academic language in your second clip.

Video Quality

Many candidates worry about the quality of their recordings. Naturally you want to submit clips in which you and your students can be seen and heard, but having said that, your quality does not have to be motion-picture perfect. In fact, you will need to compress your videos in order to submit them to Pearson, and compression can affect quality.

You are allowed to write a transcript if there are any sections in your video where you or your students cannot be heard. Also, if you are working with students who speak a language other than English or Spanish, you can translate and provide captions for the translations.

Use YouTube as a Resource

Because candidates use different technologies—various computers, recording devices, and editing software—again, visit YouTube as your resource for any questions about recording with your selected device, backing up your recordings onto a computer, clipping (but not editing) your videos, and compressing them.

For example, if you type, "How to transfer a video from my Samsung tablet onto a PC" or "How to compress video on a Mac without losing quality," you will find many instructional videos that will walk you through the process, step by step. Students are always amazed at how helpful YouTube can be when they are working with digital technologies.

Again, plan on recording ALL of your lessons, and do record them all the way through. You never know, really, how the clips will turn out, and you want to have plenty to pull from. Just remember, though, only two clips will be submitted.

Task 2—Commentary Advice

Once you have drafted your documents and templates for Task 2, use the advice below to ensure that you have done a thorough job:

- Write in the present or past tense.
- When you address the question about creating a positive learning environment, make sure that you specify how you challenged students to engage in learning.
- When you address the question about prior learning and personal, cultural, and community assets, break your response into two paragraphs and discuss how you invited students both to reference prior knowledge and to connect the learning to their lives. Quote those moments and include time stamps.
- When you address the last question about how you would revise your teaching, make sure you discuss specific places where you see the missed opportunities that led you to recommend changes. Make sure you include time stamps of where these missed opportunities occurred.
- When justifying your proposed revisions for your lessons, clearly state the changes you propose, then write why you think those changes would improve the lesson, and then write about the research/theory that supports your opinion and why.
- When addressing the question about how you deepened student learning, actually include the higher-order-thinking questions you asked and provide the time stamps. Quote yourself and students to demonstrate that you built knowledge together as a class.
- When addressing the question about engaging students and supporting them to work with some independence, name the concept/strategy/skill you are working on to remind your reader of what it is. Where in your clip can it be seen that you are supporting students to practice what you modeled? Include clips that demonstrate where your students are engaged as evidence. Describe and time stamp specific moments that prove they are engaged.
- Review the rubrics associated with each prompt and as described in this chapter to ensure that you are meeting the requirements to earn a level 3 for each question.

TASK 3

A Note about Your Focus Students and Their Assessments

If you teach in an elementary context, you will obviously use the one class you work with all day as your focus class. If you are in a secondary context, you will focus on one class and write about *just that class for the entire assessment*.

In the process of getting set up and organized, you will want to select three students from your focus class. You will be scoring summative assessments for your whole class and recording everyone's score, but you will only be submitting the actual, filled-in, and/or recorded summative assessments of your three students.

When selecting your students, choose students who represent the range of learners in your class. For example, select an advanced student (or athlete if you teach physical education), someone who struggles in some way or has an IEP, 504 plan, or another accommodation, and a student who is an English Language Learner. These would be students you have included in your Task 1, Part A, chart. If you don't have that kind of diversity in your classroom, think in terms of your A-, B-, and C-level students, and select one of each. That's a little simplistic, but hopefully you get the idea. What you want to accomplish with your focus students is to demonstrate that you can successfully work with and support a range of students.

Selecting One Assessment

For this task, you will be working with only *one assessment*. It is a good idea for this to be a summative assessment, as described throughout this book. This summative assessment will be described when you write about your assessment plans in Task 1E.

Plan to implement an assessment that allows your students to demonstrate that they have met the learning objectives you have established for your learning segment. The summative assessment can take any form (essay, conversation, debate, solving an equation, drill, poster, etc.). Whatever form you choose should be appropriate for your discipline—a logical vehicle with which your students can demonstrate their progress with the learning objectives and one that is aligned with your disciplinary standards and requirements. Review chapter 5 for advice about how to design a high-quality assessment.

You will administer the summative assessment to your whole class, you will score the summative assessment for your whole class, and you will record the scores from your whole class (see chapter 7 for a reminder about how to do this). However, you will *collect* completed assessments (work samples) from your three students only.

Part A—Student Work Samples (Word Documents, Images, Audio Files, Video Clips)

For this part, you will upload your students' completed assessments. These are their work samples.

Note that in addition to uploading your students' paper assessments, you can also use video clips or audio clips. Regardless of your discipline, including PE, it is advisable to administer paper assessments in addition to video or audio if appropriate.[5]

Plan to scan, take pictures, audio record, and/or video record your three students' completed assessments. And know that when you actually share and analyze these, you can use a variety of media to showcase these assessments.

You might use an audio recording if you are working with young children who are demonstrating their learning orally—if they are learning to read, for example. You could also use audio if your assessment includes an oral component, such as a debate in history or a presentation in health or a world language.

You may also upload short video clips (totaling five minutes for all three students) from any moment in your lessons where your students are working with the academic language requirements you identified in your Task 1 commentary, so you could upload those clips in this section as well. These might be short clips where your students are working with the language demand or vocabulary that you have highlighted for this learning segment. It's a good idea to use the same language demands that students had to work on in the summative assessment, but this is not a requirement.

Part B—Evidence of Feedback (Word Documents, Images, Audio Files, Video Clips)

For Part B, you will scan or take a picture of the feedback you give each of your three focus students described above. This should include a scored rubric or checklist, as well as comments that you write either directly on each assessment or on sticky notes, as recommended in chapter 7. If using video or audio clips for student work samples, you will provide your students with oral feedback.

Please remember that the feedback you provide your students should not be cursory or random. Your feedback must be targeted and specific. And that means that your feedback aligns with the specific learning objectives/ evaluation criteria that you established for your learning segment/summative assessment.

If you provide a lot of feedback about spelling and grammar but you have not listed those topics in your learning objectives/evaluation criteria, your feedback is not aligned. It's fine to make a note about these topics, but make certain that the majority of your feedback aligns with your learning objectives/evaluation criteria.

In other words, make sure that you do more than write comments such as "Nice!" or "Well done!" or "Use a dictionary to check your spelling!" You want your feedback to be aligned with your central focus and learning objectives and to be concrete so that students can build on it going forward and improve as well.

If you have a focus student who earned the highest possible score, provide feedback about what they might do next time to challenge themselves a bit more. For example, you might write: "The next time you write a critical essay, it might be interesting to write about connections to contemporary issues/events in your conclusion." That way you help your student think about how to further improve and how to build on those learning objectives, even if they met or even surpassed your evaluation criteria.

Part C—Assessment Commentary (Template)

This is a template that you will get from your college instructor or directly from Pearson when you register. On this template, you will upload a table that represents how your whole class did on the summative assessment.

Chapter 7 is designed to prepare you to address the prompts on this commentary. And as described in this chapter, you will need to collect the summative assessment for your entire class and record their scores. You will analyze how your whole class did in terms of your established evaluation criteria and also, how *each of your focus students did*.

You will also analyze the extent to which your class successfully worked with the academic language you highlighted in your lesson plans and your Task 1 commentary, so *make sure you deliberately include academic language work in this summative assessment*. You will describe the feedback you provided your students and, based on your analysis of how they did, you will describe the logical "next steps" that make sense as related to the skills and understandings (the learning objectives) you taught . . . and that your students learned.

Part D—Evaluation Criteria (Word Document)

Task 3, Part D, is your evaluation criteria. This was also described in chapter 7. Your evaluation criteria is the rubric or checklist that you used to score your summative assessment, and it is crucial that you set it up in a way that will help you successfully analyze your students' summative assessments.

Remember that your evaluation criteria should be a mirror of your learning objectives. You state your learning objectives when planning, and you flip those and use them as your evaluation criteria when assessing. Your evaluation criteria align with your central focus, your learning objectives, your disciplinary requirements, and the associated state/national standards.

TASK 3 CHECKLIST

Once you have selected your student work samples (with your feedback), and drafted your documents and templates for Task 3, use the checklist below to ensure that you have done a thorough job with Task 3.

- ☑ I have selected a summative assessment that measures the skills/understandings of each student in my class.
- ☑ I have selected three focus students. The focus students represent the range of students in my class, such as a student with an IEP or 504 plan, an English Language Learner, a struggling reader, an underperforming student, a student with gaps in academic knowledge, a gifted student, etc. I have made sure *not* to use language that describes them as "high performing" or "low performing."
- ☑ I have collected and scanned or photographed the summative assessment (work samples) from the three students chosen above. I have clearly labeled them (Focus Student 1 Summative Assessment), and I have saved these as either PDFs or Word documents. If using audio or video clips, I have clearly labeled and saved these files.
- ☑ If any of the focus student work is illegible, I have transcribed their work directly on the work samples.
- ☑ I have de-identified each focus student and refer to each as focus student 1, focus student 2, focus student 3.
- ☑ If I am using a video assessment, I have one clip per focus student and I have clearly identified each student on my Task 3, Part E, commentary (describing a student's hair color and shirt color for example).
- ☑ Each item on my evaluation criteria aligns with my learning objectives/ disciplinary requirements/standards.
- ☑ I have created a rubric or checklist for my evaluation criteria that I will use to score each student's summative assessment.
- ☑ I have scored the summative assessment for each individual student in my class.
- ☑ I have broken each student's score down according to the evaluation criteria so that I can create a detailed table.

- ☑ I have provided feedback for each focus student—either on a video recording, audio recording, or in writing. If using a video recording, I can clearly be seen providing feedback to the student. If my video recording is not audible, I will transcribe the feedback I provided. I will provide specific time stamps where the feedback occurs.
- ☑ I have also included at least one "glow" and one "grow" that connects with my learning objectives/evaluation criteria for each focus student.
- ☑ If I provided feedback to my focus students using audio or video feedback, I can be seen in the video providing feedback. If I cannot be heard, I have transcribed the feedback. If providing audio feedback, I can be heard on the recording. I have included three separate files for Task 3, Part B, if using video or audio. These are clearly labeled and in the correct format *audio*: (flv, asf, wmv, qt, mov, mpg, avi, mp3, wav, mp4, wma) or *video*: (flv, asf, qt, mov, mpg, mpeg, avi, wmv, mp4, m4v).

My Analysis

- ☑ When writing about the patterns of learning, I really spelled them out clearly for the reader. I described what the patterns of learning are. I described where my students generally do well or not so well. I didn't just list the numbers. I described why students generally earned those scores.
- ☑ I made sure to identify these patterns of learning as related to my disciplinary requirements (the orange squares). I actually named those disciplinary requirements in my commentary and highlighted them.
- ☑ I made sure that in my analysis of patterns of learning, I discussed my whole class and also learners who belong to certain groups: ELL or advanced students/athletes, and even individuals who stand out—like my focus students.
- ☑ I included specific evidence from the summative assessment in my evaluation of *each* focus student. I included a quote from their summative assessment that demonstrates a "glow" and a "grow."
- ☑ I made sure to address how each focus student did in terms of my learning objectives/evaluation criteria and my disciplinary requirements. In my writing commentary, I kept referring back goals and writing about each focus student in terms of those goals.

Feedback

- ☑ I briefly (one or two sentences) described what kind of learner each focus student is and what their general needs are.
- ☑ I clearly explained the kind of feedback I provided. For example, I explained if I was referencing feedback from a video and/or from the paper assessment.

☑ I clearly explained how my feedback connects to the learning objectives/evaluation criteria and also each focus student's needs.
☑ I clearly explained how I will help my focus students understand the feedback.
☑ I clearly explained how I will help each student reflect on and also set goals for *themselves* (in addition to the goals I recommended to them).
☑ I clearly explained how each student can use the feedback in a new learning opportunity/project that builds on what they learned.

Academic Language Demands

☑ I clearly explained what evidence I was referencing to describe how my students did with the language demands (for example, if I used a video clip and the summative assessment as evidence).
☑ I focused on ONE language function. I stated it and described how well (or not so well) my students worked with this.
☑ I organized my responses around the language demands, writing at least one paragraph for each topic (one for the language function, one for vocabulary, one for discourse, etc.).
☑ I wrote something to the effect of "This is what students did with the language function, and this is how they did with the language function . . . this is what they did with the vocabulary on the assessment, and this is how they did with the vocabulary, this is what they did with the discourse, and this is how they did with the discourse, etc."
☑ I described what my students generally did well with or struggled with for each language demand.

Next Steps

☑ I explained how I will have my class apply this new learning to a different unit.
☑ I clearly explained how, specifically, I will support them to revisit the learning objectives that they struggled with.
☑ I listed the learning objectives/evaluation criteria that my "next steps" connect to.
☑ I wrote individual "next steps" for each focus student and explained why they are appropriate (and connected to my learning objectives/evaluation criteria).
☑ I included "next steps" that my students (whole class and then each individual focus student) need more support with and also an idea about how to apply what they learned to a new unit—the next—of study.
☑ I differentiated the "next steps" for each of my focus students.

☑ I made sure to explain how my "next steps" connect directly to the analysis I have done when addressing the other questions in this commentary. In other words, I clearly explain how the assessment results led me to propose these "next steps." I made strong connections to my learning objectives and how students did in terms of those.

Elementary candidates: See the references chapter for support with Task 4.

How Is the EdTPA Scored?

For the three tasks, most handbooks have fifteen rubrics affiliated with them, five rubrics per task. Elementary education candidates will have eighteen rubrics.[6] Your scorer does not directly evaluate your artifacts; they will reference those artifacts for evidence that what you write in your templates is accurate, and to get further insight into your work if needed.

The rubrics themselves align with the questions you will answer on the templates (Task 1, Part E; Task 2, Part B; and Task 3, Part C.) There will be some variety among handbooks, however. For example, Task 4 for elementary candidates will include an additional three rubrics. Each participating state publishes information about passing scores for each handbook.

Below is some final advice from former student teachers who scored well on the edTPA. They were each asked to reflect on their edTPA work and make a recommendation about how to earn a high score to future student teachers. The advice has been organized consecutively, from Task 1 through Task 3.

TASK 1

- Ensure that your plans are aligned with your central focus, standards, and your specific disciplinary requirements. And make certain that there are no content inaccuracies in your plans.
- Make sure that you clearly state how each of your lesson plans builds on the next so that, together, they help students develop both the understandings and skills that connect with your central focus and help your students build this learning toward your summative assessment.
- Make sure you do a thorough job describing how your planned supports are appropriate for your whole class (their prior learning, interests, developmental needs, and any other supports that your whole group might need), groups of students (such as your ELLs, a group of struggling readers, or a group of advanced students for example), and individuals (classified students or individuals who need specific supports just for them).

- If you list a classified student on your chart on the Task 1, Part A, template, you must address how you planned to support that student's learning.
- Make sure that you justify why your plans connect with both your students' prior learning and their interests/assets.
- Clearly explain how you know your plans connect with prior learning and student interests/assets.
- Choose a theorist or researcher whom you have met in one of your methods classes, and explain why that theorist would agree with your plans.
- Know that when you write about how your plans connect with your particular students, if you don't provide a strong justification, it does not matter how well you discuss that connection, so put more effort into your justification than into your connection to theory/research.
- When you write about your academic language plans, clearly describe the language function you have selected, and describe how your students will practice working with it. Then describe how the other language demands—vocabulary, discourse, and syntax—help support your students to work with your language function.
- Make sure to describe how the language demands you write about in Task 1 are used in the service of the language function that you have identified as your larger, central focus.
- Make sure that you describe each assessment that you plan to use in your learning segment. For each assessment you describe, make sure you *clearly state what evidence of learning each assessment will provide you*. And when you do so, make sure that each assessment you describe provides evidence of learning that is discipline-specific—in other words, aligned with your disciplinary requirements.
- Demonstrate that your assessments provide your students with multiple opportunities and multiple ways to demonstrate that they are meeting the learning objectives you have established for them.

TASK 2

- Do not reference moments that cannot be observed in your video clips, and make sure that if you make a claim about what you did in your video, you provide a time stamp as evidence.
- It's okay if your students are not perfectly behaved, but don't use a clip if the environment is disruptive to the point that students are not able to learn. So if one or more students consistently interfere with the learning of others, choose another clip to submit.

- If you are acting in a way that is disrespectful (like an authoritarian who is mean to students), you will not pass, and if you tolerate students being disrespectful to you or each other, you will not pass.
- Include clips that demonstrate respect with and among your students, and that your classroom is "low-risk," or "emotionally safe," meaning students seem comfortable enough to share their ideas and ask questions when they are confused.
- Choose clips that show you have engaged your students in the disciplinary requirements explained in your handbook, not just in random activities. Clearly state how the engagement connects with those requirements.
- Elicit responses from your students that demonstrate that they are thinking deeply about the disciplinary requirements of your handbook. In other words, they are working with higher-order-thinking questions in relation to your learning objectives. You do not need to show in your clips that students are working with *all* of your disciplinary requirements, just some of them.
- Demonstrate that you have provided your students with subject-specific methods to help your students learn your discipline. For example, if you are working with literacy, your clips demonstrate that you model a literacy strategy for your students. If you are working in math, you demonstrate that you used representations to help students understand the content.
- Demonstrate that you supported your students to engage in learning activities themselves, fostering some independence.
- Demonstrate that you can provide instruction that connects to the conceptual understandings of your discipline; don't just focus on surface skills, such as facts.
- Identify specific moments in your clips that you think were "missed opportunities" to better support and/or challenge the majority or groups of your students. These proposed changes should be evident in the clips and they should be related to your learning objectives rather than surface-level changes, such as what color markers you used on the whiteboard. Strive to write about places in your clips where individuals could have been better supported or challenged.

TASK 3

- Make certain that the evaluation criteria you establish do indeed address your disciplinary requirements—align with your learning objectives and standards as well.

- Ensure that your analysis of your students' summative assessment results is not only aligned, but that your analysis addresses more than superficial performance, such as spelling and grammar.
- In addition to describing the patterns of learning that you see when you analyze your class performance, you want to include a description of some of the differences you notice among your students.
- If the majority of your students did well in regard to one of your criteria, that might be a general pattern of learning that you can address; but if a handful did not do well, make sure you include that in your analysis also.
- Make sure you include specific evidence in your analysis, so pull quotes from your focus students' work to support your analysis.
- Make sure the feedback you provide your students is connected to your central focus and that it is correct—no content mistakes.
- Your feedback should be very specific. For example, if one learning objective for a history paper is for students to clearly explain the three challenges faced by Lewis and Clark on their expedition and to support the explanation with textual evidence, general feedback might look like this: "Good, clear argument." That is obviously general. However, if you write, "Good job articulating three challenges faced by the Lewis and Clark expedition. I thought your description of their navigational challenge was especially interesting, accurate, and well-supported." That is much more specific.
- Clearly explain how you will support students to both *understand* and *apply* the feedback you provided.
- Write about how you will help students apply the feedback. And don't just write about the feedback that addresses what students did wrong. Address what your students did well also, and write about how you will help students build on what they did well going forward.
- Provide different feedback (rather than just generic comments) for each of your three focus students; that is a good idea, and it demonstrates that you are taking the specific learning needs of each focus student into account.
- Remember that your plan to help students understand and apply the feedback must align with your learning objectives. Don't spend time addressing topics that do not connect with those objectives.
- When you write about how well students did with the academic language on your summative assessments, try to describe how they did with at least three language demands. How well did they work with vocabulary? Syntax or discourse? Some handbooks, such as English as an Additional Language and Secondary Math have other language requirements, so review those in your handbook.
- Remember that you are explaining and giving evidence of your students' work with the academic language. You don't have to prove that they mas-

tered it, so it is fine to describe and provide evidence of both their success and places where they fell short.
- Explain how your "next steps" connect to your analysis of the assessment. Don't just make up random "next steps." You must connect them to how your whole group of students did on the summative assessment and how your individuals did as well.
- Connect your "next steps" to your disciplinary requirements and your learning objectives/evaluation criteria.
- Make sure that your "next steps" are specific to the learning, not just general.
- The more aligned your "next steps" are with your central focus, the better. The more specific they are, the better. And the more individualized they are, the better they will be.
- When you write "next steps," make certain that you address the students you listed on your 1A chart.

REFLECTING ON THE CHAPTER

After reviewing the chapter, consider what aspects of the edTPA seem most challenging. Make a note of those so that you can revisit those topics in this chapter, use your edTPA handbook and other resources for additional support, and pose questions to your mentors. Also, when you examine those topics that seem most daunting, consider who might be able to help you work through them. And don't forget about other candidates preparing for the edTPA. Having a strong support system will be crucial.

NOTES

1. Because there are many different edTPA handbooks (for different disciplines) and each one is unique, this chapter and this book address common requirements; some handbooks will have additional, specific requirements, so it will be important for all candidates to consult their handbooks.
2. Board of Trustees of the Leland Stanford Junior University (2016).
3. You can use a formative assessment for Task 3, but it is recommended that you use a summative assessment so that you have plenty to write about. See chapter 5.
4. "edTPA Guidelines for Acceptable Candidate Support," Stanford Center for Assessment, Learning & Equity (revised September 2016), https://www.edtpa.com/content/docs/guidelinesforsupportingcandidates.pdf.
5. Some disciplines, such as physical education, must include a video work sample for their focus students.
6. Please see the references for a resource that will support your work with Task 4.

References

Supporting Your Student Teaching with Further Reading

RESOURCES FOR CHAPTER 1: PLANNING FOR A SUCCESSFUL STUDENT TEACHING EXPERIENCE

Cox, Janelle, "A Student Teaching Survival Guide," TeachHUB, accessed January 31, 2019, https://www.teachhub.com/student-teaching-survival-guide.

Love, Teach, "7 Habits of Amazing Student Teachers," WeAreTeachers, accessed January 31, 2019, https://www.weareteachers.com/7-habits-of-amazing-student-teachers/.

MacDonald, Colla J., "Coping with Stress during the Teaching Practicum: The Student Teacher's Perspective," ResearchGate, accessed January 31, 2019, https://www.researchgate.net/publication/232586505_Coping_with_stress_during_the_teaching_practicum_The_student_teacher's_perspective.

Varlas, Laura, "Ten Survival Tips from a Student Teacher," ASCD Education Update, accessed January 31, 2019, http://www.ascd.org/publications/newsletters/education-update/dec16/vol58/num12/Ten-Survival-Tips-from-a-Student-Teacher.aspx.

Vito, Sam, "10 Stages of Student Teaching," *Odyssey*, April 14, 2017, https://www.theodysseyonline.com/10-stages-of-student-teaching.

RESOURCES FOR CHAPTER 2: WORKING WITH YOUR PROGRAM-BASED MENTORS

Cox, Janelle, "Student Teacher Observation Checklist," ThoughtCo, accessed January 31, 2019, https://www.thoughtco.com/student-teacher-observation-checklist-2081421.

TeachThought Staff, "Looming Teacher Observation? 7 Tips For A Better Outcome," TeachThought (blog), January 26, 2015, https://www.teachthought.com/pedagogy/looming-teacher-observation-7-tips-better-outcome/.

RESOURCES FOR CHAPTER 3: WORKING WITH KEY SCHOOL STAKEHOLDERS

Your Cooperating Teacher

Ganser, Tom, "The Cooperating Teacher Role," *The Teacher Educator* 31, no. 4 (March 1, 1996): 283–91, https://doi.org/10.1080/08878739609555121.

Matsko, Kavita Kapadia, et al., "Cooperating Teacher as Model and Coach: What Leads to Student Teachers' Perceptions of Preparedness?" *Journal of Teacher Education* (August 1, 2018), 0022487118791992, https://doi.org/10.1177/0022487118791992.

Rajuan, Maureen, Douwe Beijaard, and Nico Verloop, "The Role of the Cooperating Teacher: Bridging the Gap between the Expectations of Cooperating Teachers and Student Teachers," *Mentoring & Tutoring: Partnership in Learning* 15, no. 3 (August 1, 2007): 223–42, https://doi.org/10.1080/13611260701201703.

School Personnel

Johnson, Ben, "Five Ways to Develop a Partnership with Your Principal," Edutopia, accessed January 31, 2019, https://www.edutopia.org/blog/teacher-principal-partnerships-ben-johnson.

Meador, Derrick, "A Comprehensive Breakdown of the Roles of School Personnel," ThoughtCo, accessed January 31, 2019, https://www.thoughtco.com/a-comprehensive-breakdown-of-the-roles-of-school-personnel-3194684.

———, "How Teachers Can Build a Trusting Relationship with Their Principal," ThoughtCo, accessed January 31, 2019, https://www.thoughtco.com/build-a-trusting-relationship-with-their-principal-3194349.

Getting Along with School Personnel

Fast, R. B., "What You Can Do to End Teacher Gossip," Bee Line Consulting, LLC (blog), August 30, 2017, https://beelineconsulting.net/teacher-gossip/.

Mulvahill, Elizabeth, "How to Handle Workplace Gossip Like a Champ," WeAreTeachers, January 12, 2017, https://www.weareteachers.com/workplace-gossip/.

Powell, Lauren, "Why I Avoid the 'Teachers' Lounge and You Should, Too," *Education Week Teacher*, accessed January 31, 2019, https://www.edweek.org/tm/articles/2016/08/09/why-i-avoid-the-teachers-lounge-and.html.

Avoid Gossiping about Students

Marx-Talarczyk, JoAnna, "Five Things Teachers Should Know about Student Privacy," Special Report, InsideTheSchool, accessed January 31, 2019, https://www.russell.k12.ky.us/userfiles/indexblue/FiveStudentPrivacy.pdf.

Building Relationships with Students

Boynton, Mark, and Christine Boynton, "Chapter 1. Developing Positive Teacher-Student Relations," ASCD Books, accessed January 31, 2019, http://www.ascd.

org/publications/books/105124/chapters/Developing_Positive_Teacher-Student_Relations.aspx.

Brown, Tara, "The Power of Positive Relationships," AMLE—Association for Middle Level Education, accessed January 31, 2019, https://www.amle.org/BrowsebyTopic/WhatsNew/WNDet/TabId/270/ArtMID/888/ArticleID/185/The-Power-of-Positive-Relationships.aspx.

Connell, Genia, "10 Ways to Build Relationships with Students this Year," *Scholastic*, accessed January 31, 2019, https://www.scholastic.com/teachers/blog-posts/genia-connell/10-ways-build-relationships-students-year-1/.

Denton, Paula, *The Power of Our Words: Teacher Language That Helps Children Learn*, 2nd edition, edited by Lynn Bechtel (Turners Falls, MA: Center for Responsive Schools, 2013).

Goodman, Stacey, "The Importance of Teaching through Relationships," Edutopia, accessed January 31, 2019, https://www.edutopia.org/blog/importance-teaching-through-relationships-stacey-goodman.

Sears, Nina, "Building Relationships with Students," National Education Association (NEA), accessed January 31, 2019, http://www.nea.org/tools/29469.htm.

"TED Talks Education: 'Build Relationships with Your Students,'" PBS LearningMedia, accessed January 31, 2019, https://ny.pbslearningmedia.org/resource/83f0beff-a14a-434d-b551-4b53e3dee640/ted-talks-education-build-relationships-with-your-students/.

Establishing Relationships with Parents

Aguilar, Elena, "20 Tips for Developing Positive Relationships with Parents," Edutopia, accessed January 31, 2019, https://www.edutopia.org/blog/20-tips-developing-positive-relationships-parents-elena-aguilar.

Brantley, Danielle, "Five Ways Teachers Can Establish Positive Relationships with Parents," Teach.com (blog), August 20, 2018, https://teach.com/blog/five-ways-teachers-can-establish-positive-relationships-with-parents/.

"Effective Communication with Parents," *Education World*, accessed January 31, 2019, https://www.educationworld.com/a_admin/effective-communication-with-parents.shtml.

"New Teacher Survival Guide: The Parent-Teacher Conference," Teaching Channel, September 1, 2011, https://www.teachingchannel.org/video/parent-teacher-conference-tips.

RESOURCES FOR CHAPTER 4: DESIGNING HIGH-QUALITY LESSON PLANS

The Central Focus

Overholt, Drew, "A Guide to the edTPA's Central Focus and Academic Language Sections, With Examples," Owlcation, accessed January 31, 2019, https://owlcation.com/academia/edTPA-Help-Central-Focus-and-Academic-Language.

Resources to Help You Differentiate Your Instruction

Marzano, Robert J., "The Art and Science of Teaching: A Comprehensive Framework for Effective Instruction," *Choice Reviews Online* 45, no. 11 (July 1, 2008): 45-6316-45–6316, https://doi.org/10.5860/CHOICE.45-6316.

"Page 4: Differentiate Instructional Elements," IrisCenter, accessed January 31, 2019, https://iris.peabody.vanderbilt.edu/module/di/cresource/q2/p04/.

Raffaelli, Lina, "18 Teacher-Tested Strategies for Differentiated Instruction," Edutopia, accessed January 31, 2019, https://www.edutopia.org/discussion/18-teacher-tested-strategies-differentiated-instruction.

"Reach Every Student through Differentiated Instruction," Reach Every Student, Ontario, accessed January 31, 2019, http://www.edugains.ca/resourcesDI/Brochures/DIBrochureOct08.pdf.

Strom, Erich, "The Difference between Accommodations and Modifications," Understood.org, accessed January 31, 2019, https://www.understood.org/en/learning-attention-issues/treatments-approaches/educational-strategies/the-difference-between-accommodations-and-modifications.

TeachThought Staff, "10 Examples & Non-Examples of Differentiated Instruction," TeachThought (blog), September 26, 2014, https://www.teachthought.com/pedagogy/what-is-differentiated-instruction/.

Wu, Echo H., "The Path Leading to Differentiation: An Interview with Carol Tomlinson," *Journal of Advanced Academics* 24, no. 2 (May 1, 2013): 125–33, https://doi.org/10.1177/1932202X13483472.

Resources to Help You with Academic Language

"Academic Language Gridv3.Pdf," accessed January 31, 2019, https://www.wpunj.edu/coe/departments/field/assets/Academic%20Language%20Gridv3.pdf.

Finley, Todd, "8 Strategies for Teaching Academic Language," Edutopia, January 2, 2014, https://www.edutopia.org/blog/8-strategies-teaching-academic-language-todd-finley.

Freiberger, Scott B., "Academic Language Matters," Language Magazine (blog), July 17, 2017, https://www.languagemagazine.com/2017/07/17/academic-language-matters/.

Gottlieb, Margo, and Gisela Ernst-Slavit, "A Centerpiece for Academic Success in English Language Arts," in *Academic Language in Diverse Classrooms: English Language Arts, Grades 6–8: Promoting Content and Language Learning*, edited by M. Gottlieb and G. Ernst-Slavit (Thousand Oaks, CA: Corwin, 2014), 44.

Denton, David, "Academic Language for EdTPA," accessed January 31, 2019, https://www.youtube.com/watch?v=HcEqbeVNPqQ.

———, "PassedTPA: Strategies for Passing edTPA: Academic Language Simplified," accessed January 31, 2019, http://www.passedtpa.com/hello-world/.

"What Are Language Functions?" ELD Strategies, accessed January 31, 2019, http://eldstrategies.com/languagefunctions.html.

Zwiers, Jeff, *Building Academic Language: Meeting Common Core Standards across Disciplines, Grades 5–12*, 2nd edition (San Francisco: Wiley & Sons, 2014), 15.

Zwiers, Jeff, and Marie Crawford, *Academic Conversations: Classroom Talk that Fosters Critical Thinking and Content Understandings* (Portsmouth, NH: Stenhouse, 2010), accessed January 31, 2019, https://www.stenhouse.com/content/academic-conversations.

Resources to Help You Find Theorists

Heick, Terry, "A Visual Summary: 32 Learning Theories Every Teacher Should Know," accessed January 31, 2019, https://www.teachthought.com/learning/a-visual-summary-the-most-important-learning-theories/.
Illeris, Knud, *Contemporary Theories of Learning* (London, New York: Routledge, 2009).
"Learning Theories and Models Summaries," *Educational Psychology*," accessed January 31, 2019, https://www.learning-theories.com/.
"Major Theories and Models of Learning," *Educational Psychology*," accessed January 31, 2019, https://courses.lumenlearning.com/educationalpsychology/chapter/major-theories-and-models-of-learning/.
"Sample Lesson Plans," https://docs.google.com/document/d/1Y3EdN-TlaRI_jep-685w4jL-Bv8lsQAUvijKNMEXc9co/edit?usp=sharing.
"6 Education Theorists All Teachers Should Know Infographic," Teacher Infographics, e-Learning Infographics, December 7, 2015, https://elearninginfographics.com/6-education-theorists-teachers-know-infographic/.
Zhou, Molly, and David Brown, *Educational Learning Theories*, 2nd edition (Education Open Textbooks, 2015), 129.

RESOURCES FOR CHAPTER 5: DESIGNING A RANGE OF HIGH-QUALITY ASSESSMENTS

Different Kinds of Assessments

TeachThought Staff, "6 Types of Assessment of Learning," TeachThought (blog), January 25, 2018, https://www.teachthought.com/pedagogy/6-types-assessment-learning/.

Pre-Assessment

Es, Harvey Scot, "Pre-Assessment Strategies," n.d., 1.
Guskey, Thomas R., "Does Pre-Assessment Work?," *Educational Leadership* 75, no. 5 (February 2018): 8.
Pendergrass, Emily, "Differentiation: It Starts with Pre-Assessment," *Educational Leadership* 71, no. 4 (December 2013/January 2014), accessed January 31, 2019, http://www.ascd.org/publications/educational_leadership/dec13/vol71/num04/Differentiation@_It_Starts_with_Pre-Assessment.aspx.

"Six Traits of Quality Pre-Assessments," Byrdseed.com (blog), accessed January 31, 2019, https://www.byrdseed.com/six-traits-of-quality-pre-assessments/.

Stockman, Angela, "10 Creative Pre-Assessment Ideas You May Not Know," Brilliant or Insane: Education on the Edge (blog), April 26, 2015, http://www.brilliantinsane.com/2015/04/10-creative-pre-assessment-ideas-you-may-not-know.html.

Formative Assessment

"Benefits of Formative Assessment: What Is Formative Assessment?" National Council of Teachers of Mathematics, accessed January 31, 2019, https://www.nctm.org/Research-and-Advocacy/Research-Brief-and-Clips/Benefits-of-Formative-Assessment/.

Dodge, Judith, "What Are Formative Assessments and Why Should We Use Them?" *Scholastic*, accessed January 31, 2019, https://www.scholastic.com/teachers/articles/teaching-content/what-are-formative-assessments-and-why-should-we-use-them/.

Greenstein, Laura, "Chapter 1: The Fundamentals of Formative Assessment," in *What Teachers Really Need to Know about Formative Assessment*, accessed January 31, 2019, http://www.ascd.org/publications/books/110017/chapters/The-Fundamentals-of-Formative-Assessment.aspx.

Scherer, Marge, *On Formative Assessment: Readings from Educational Leadership (EL Essentials)* (ASCD, 2016), http://public.eblib.com/choice/publicfullrecord.aspx?p=4625385.

Watanabe-Crockett, Lee, "10 Innovative Formative Assessment Examples for Teachers to Know," Global Digital Citizen Foundation (blog), April 18, 2018, https://globaldigitalcitizen.org/10-innovative-formative-assessment-examples.

Wees, David, "56 Examples of Formative Assessment," Edutopia, accessed January 31, 2019, https://www.edutopia.org/groups/assessment/250941.

Summative Assessment

Burke, Kay, *Balanced Assessment: From Formative to Summative* (Bloomington, IN: Solution Tree, 2010).

Carnegie Mellon University, "What Is the Difference between Formative and Summative Assessment?" Eberly Center, Carnegie Mellon University, accessed January 31, 2019, https://www.cmu.edu/teaching/assessment/basics/formative-summative.html.

CCEA, "What Is Summative Assessment?" CCEA (Council for the Curriculum, Examinations, and Assessment), November 16, 2015, http://ccea.org.uk/curriculum/assess_progress/types_assessment/summative.

Lynch, Matthew, "The Five Major Features of Summative Assessments," The Edvocate (blog), November 22, 2016, https://www.theedadvocate.org/five-major-features-summative-assessments/.

Reddy, Krishna, "Summative Evaluation—Top 22 Advantages and Disadvantages," WiseStep (blog), June 22, 2016, https://content.wisestep.com/advantages-disadvantages-summative-evaluation/.

Creating Rubrics

Brown University, "Designing Grading Rubrics," https://www.brown.edu/sheridan/teaching-learning-resources/teaching-resources/course-design/classroom-assessment/grading-criteria/designing-rubrics.

RESOURCES FOR CHAPTER 6: DESIGNING HIGH-QUALITY INSTRUCTION

Creating a Positive Learning Environment

"Classroom Management: A Collection of Resources for Teachers," Scholastic, accessed January 31, 2019, https://www.scholastic.com/teachers/collections/teaching-content/classroom-management-collection-resources-teachers/.

Erwin, Jonathan C., "10 Ways Teachers Can Create a Positive Learning Environment," Free Spirit Publishing (blog), November 29, 2016, https://freespiritpublishingblog.com/2016/11/29/ten-ways-teachers-can-create-a-positive-learning-environment/.

Lynch, Matthew, "5 Must Have Classroom Management Apps, Tools, and Resources," The Tech Edvocate (blog), October 15, 2017, https://www.thetechedvocate.org/5-must-classroom-management-apps-tools-resources/.

"32 Strategies for Building a Positive Learning Environment," Edutopia, accessed January 31, 2019, https://www.edutopia.org/discussion/32-strategies-building-positive-learning-environment.

"ASCD Book: Better Than Carrots or Sticks: Restorative Practices for Positive Classroom Management," accessed January 31, 2019, http://www.ascd.org/Publications/Books/Overview/Better-Than-Carrots-or-Sticks.aspx.

"THE Classroom Management Book: Harry K. Wong, Rosemary T. Wong, Sarah F. Jondahl, Oretha F. Ferguson, Various, N/A: 8601418270096: Amazon.Com: Books," accessed January 31, 2019, https://www.amazon.com/Classroom-Management-Book-Harry-Wong/dp/0976423332.

RESOURCES FOR CHAPTER 8: COMPOSING A STRONG, ALIGNED EDTPA

A Table for Most Disciplinary Requirements with Translations and Examples

"Working with Disciplinary Requirements: Your Disciplinary Requirements," https://docs.google.com/document/d/1YDJ6jRtXPESPZE2JFjLkaSFc0YU-ZUvN6NE0gayKA58/edit?usp=sharing.

A Breakdown of Task 4 for Elementary Education Candidates

"Task 4," https://docs.google.com/document/d/1BnJlSBcdwWKoGAcrdb7zIzG2Hy ZYgmVf4oiPTlz2sik/edit?usp=sharing.

About the Author

Trace Lahey is a teacher educator living in New York State. Trace has served as a teacher, athletic coach, and administrator in a range of educational settings. She has taught at both the elementary and secondary levels. Trace has also served as a clinical professor, working intensely with student teachers. Trace currently serves as the Education Department Chairperson at Manhattan College, where she teaches foundations and methods courses and continues to work with student teachers. Her research interests include student teaching, literacy in the content areas, and integrating creative methods in the classroom.

www.ingramcontent.com/pod-product-compliance
Lightning Source LLC
Chambersburg PA
CBHW022013300426
44117CB00005B/166